FROM
SLAVERY
TO
SONSHIP

FROM SLAVERY TO SONSHIP

A Study of Paul's Message to the Galatians

JERRY JONES

CHRISTIAN COMMUNICATIONS
P.O.BOX 150
NASHVILLE, TN 37202

FROM SLAVERY TO SONSHIP

Copyright © 1989 by Gospel Advocate Co.

All Scripture quotations are from the Holy Bible New
International Version, Copyright © 1978, New York Bible
Society, unless otherwise noted. Used by permission.

Published by Gospel Advocate Co.
P.O. Box 150, Nashville, TN 37202

ISBN 0-89225-353-3

A NOTE ABOUT
THE AUTHOR

by Clifton L. Ganus, Jr.
Chancellor, Harding University

I am very happy that Jerry Jones has written a new book entitled *From Slavery to Sonship*. He is a very capable and dedicated person and his training, insight and experience have prepared him well for this publication. I know it will be a blessing to God's people and look forward to reading it.

For the past two years, I have corresponded with Jerry, talked with him on the phone and visited with him and Claudette personally on different occasions. I have been impressed with his balance, sense of direction and desire to serve the Lord and his people in an effective and Biblical way. I wholeheartedly recommend him and his work to all who would be enlightened and inspired to do a better job in God's service.

DEDICATION

I entered Harding University (then Harding College) as a freshman Bible major in September 1956. With much eagerness, I sought to learn everything I could about the Bible and how to preach its message. I seized every opportunity to preach, even making opportunities to preach. My enthusiasm and zeal were obvious, as was my lack of knowledge of the Word and how to preach it.

During this time, God brought a brother into my life who was destined to have a great impact on me. He was a farmboy, small in stature but big in heart, from the plains of Kansas. His love for God and others quickly drew us together. He saw my sincere desire to be a man of God and a preacher of His Word. In his humble manner, this Kansas farmboy had a talk with me that changed my life. In the course of the conversation he said, "Jones, I can't preach, but I know how it's supposed to sound." With a twinkle in his eye and love in his heart, he informed me of my need to improve my "sound." Recognizing that need, I asked for his help.

Since he was an excellent song leader, we became an evangelistic team. He was also my "Barnabas," helping me develop my talents as we traveled to small Arkansas churches in the spring of 1957. During that summer, we sold Bibles for Southwestern Bible Company and continued working as a team, serving small churches in North Carolina. When he was through with the song service and it was time for me to preach, he would take out his pen and paper and listen for mistakes. Once I saw him writing before I began preaching. After the sermon, he told me it was best to walk, not run, to the pulpit! He became so proficient at catching my mistakes that he wrote them down in advance of the sermon and simply put tally marks after them in order to keep up. I made grammatical errors faster than he could write. After every sermon, we had a private debriefing. He would always begin these sessions with, "Jones, you did a great job, but. . . ." Neither my high-school teachers nor my family had adequately prepared me in the "King's English," but my friend did.

The high point of my in-the-field training came one time when I was preaching and my friend was feverishly taking notes on my mistakes. I made a glaring error, but much to his surprise, I caught it, corrected it, and went on. He nearly dropped his pencil and, with a startled look, glanced up from his paper to see if I were the one preaching. I proudly looked at him, flashed a smile, and knew I had made an *A* on that sermon.

We returned to Harding University for our sophomore year in the fall of 1957. I remember the night we drove to Harding and entered the student center filled with our old friends. However, the night was shattered when we learned that our friend, Charles Burkes, had been killed on his way to school. Charlie had been an inspiration to all of us because of his love for God and his knowledge of the Word.

Our sophomore year was filled with more traveling

and preaching. My friend remained faithful to his commitment to help me become my best for God.

After graduation in 1960, we had a chance to work together in Memphis. He was educational director for Coleman Avenue Church of Christ and I was going to Harding Graduate School of Bible and Religion, but we still found time to be together in social and religious settings. In fact, we did the first (to my knowledge) four-night meeting designed for young people in the brotherhood.

After Memphis, we were separated by miles but never in heart. I have watched my friend walk on the mountaintops and in the valleys, always praising God. He is always there for counsel, advice, or encouragement. It gives me great pleasure to dedicate this book to a friend whom I will never forget. Many people have helped me in my efforts to serve God, but he was God-sent at a special time in my life. This dedication is just a small token of my appreciation of and love for him. I will always be proud to say, "He's my friend." Whatever good I have been able to do or yet will do can be traced to this Kansas farmboy who loved me enough to patiently help me grow in the Lord.

To John Marvin Maple (better known to me as Mike, just as I am better known to him as ol' Jones), I dedicate this book. Mike, thank you for touching my life and the lives of others. Eternity will be a richer experience for many because you have lived.

PREFACE

In the summer of 1987, I began studying Galatians. After reading a few commentaries, I listened to a set of tapes by one of my former students, Larry James, and was so challenged that I desired to study more. I read other books and listened to tapes by Prentice Meador, Lynn Anderson, and Glenn Owens. My understanding of Galatians was becoming more and more relevant. For a year, I immersed myself in everything I could find to help me better understand Galatians.

The more I studied, the more I realized how little I knew. I discovered ideas, insights, and concepts that had eluded me before. A self-examination revealed how little study I actually had done in this book. Wondering why I had missed the message of Galatians in spite of all my class work, I concluded: (1) Galatians must not be as "preachable" as are other books, and (2) Galatians is usually offered as a package with Romans. Therefore, Galatians is never touched, since most teachers don't even finish Romans. Although I had an overall view, I didn't have an in-depth understanding of it.

This book isn't an in-depth or scholarly study of Galatians; some critical problems of scholarship will not be dealt with in the manner that they deserve.

My purpose here is to help you understand the true gospel and be able to recognize the counterfeit.

My sources have not always been properly noted for a number of reasons. The tapes I've heard and the books I've read have been forged into my thinking to such a degree that I either don't know or have forgotten where one ends and another begins. If material is quoted but not noted, please accept my apology. It isn't an attempt to steal from anyone. My only desire is to see the message explained and received by all.

The research was done over a twelve-month period. However, the bulk of the rough draft was written during a five-day span on a houseboat tied to a deserted island on the Mississippi near St. Peters, Missouri. I dedicated these five days to studying, writing, and praying over this book. It was an experience that I will long remember.

The information in Galatians was one of the "prime movers" in the Reformation movement during the sixteenth century. Martin Luther was so intrigued by Galatians that he referred to it as "my Kathrine" (his wife). I don't know what that did for his marriage, but I have refrained from calling it "my Claudette" (my wife).

My feelings, emotions, and understandings have undergone a change because of this study. It's impossible for me to summarize my feelings about what I have learned. However, I can summarize my study by saying, "Galatians teaches what I had always hoped was true!" It's my prayer that you will praise God (Galatians 1:24) after you read the book and that joy will possess your life (Galatians 5:22) as you look forward to eternity with God and the redeemed of all ages who have been saved by grace!

OUTLINE OF GALATIANS

I. Introduction to the Letter (1:1-10)
  A. Paul Explains His Authority (1:1-5)
     1. "Paul, an apostle" (1:1a)
     2. Paul declared the resurrection (1:1b)
     3. "And all the brothers with me" (1:2a)
     4. "To the churches in Galatia" (1:2b)
     5. The greeting (1:3)
     6. Redemptive work of Christ (1:4)
     7. Doxology (1:5)
  B. Paul and the False Teachers (1:6-10)
     1. The Galatians' defection (1:6-7a)
     2. The false teachers' heresy (1:7b-9)
     3. Attack on Paul's integrity (1:10)

II. Apostle of Liberty (1:11–2:21)
  A. Apostle by Divine Approval (1:11-24)
     1. The source of his message was divine (1:11-12)
     2. His conversion was of God (1:13-24)
  B. Apostle by Human Approval (2:1-10)
     1. Paul met with Jerusalem leaders (2:1-2)
     2. An incident concerning Titus (2:3-5)
     3. Paul's relationship with the Jerusalem apostles (2:6-10)
  C. Apostle by Action (2:11-21)

INTRODUCTION

God's Vision for the World

The very nature of God becomes evident when the promise of salvation by grace unfolds in Scripture. Even before the promise to Abraham (Genesis 12:1-3), God's gracious and forgiving nature is revealed. God's nature is to forgive, not to punish. His willingness to save the wicked cities of Sodom and Gomorrah for ten righteous people shows His intent was to save, not to destroy. However, the story of Sodom and Gomorrah does teach that God will punish when His people become perverse. "In the fourth generation your descendants will come back here, for the sin of the Amorites has not yet reached its full measure" (Genesis 15:16).

One of the classic illustrations of God's benevolent nature is revealed in Jonah. God had commanded Jonah to preach a simple message to the Assyrians in Nineveh: "Forty more days and Nineveh will be overturned" (Jonah 3:4). The people reacted to Jonah's message and repented (Jonah 3:5-9). His message didn't contain a provision for changing God's mind, but God was so moved that He decided not to destroy them (Jonah 3:10). Jonah's reaction to God's change in plans is surprising.

But Jonah was greatly displeased and became angry. He prayed to the LORD, "O LORD, is this not what I said when I was still at home? That is why I was so quick to flee to Tarshish. I knew that you are a gracious and compassionate God, slow to anger and abounding in love, a God who relents from sending calamity. Now, O LORD, take away my life, for it is better for me to die than to live" (Jonah 4:1-3).

Jonah was amazed and upset with the gracious actions of God. The last "Jonah attitude" hasn't died! Seeing God as forgiving and compassionate is equally hard for the twentieth-century man, who lives in an unforgiving society, to grasp.

Two lessons from the ministry of Jesus continued to reveal God's graciousness. The first lesson is found in Matthew 20:1-16 where the kingdom of heaven is likened to a vineyard. The owner hired workers at different hours of the day and, at the end of the day, determined to pay each person the same, regardless of how long he had worked. Some of the workers were upset with the owner's decision, and Jesus responded to this attitude. In the parable Jesus quoted the owner as saying, "Friend, I am not being unfair to you. Did you agree to work for a denarius? Take your pay and go. I want to give the man who was hired last the same as I gave you. Don't I have the right to do what I want with my own money? Or are you envious because I am generous?" (Matthew 20:13-15).

The second lesson is in Luke 15:1-32. This beautiful story of God's love for the lost is filled with a God who seeks to forgive, receive, and restore any who have left Him. God is shown as being full of compassion, running to those in need: "But while he was still a long way off, his father saw him and was filled with compassion for him; he ran to his son, threw his arms around him and kissed him" (Luke 15:20). It's hard for the legalistic, self-righteous Pharisee to accept the gracious, forgiving nature of God. The older brother in the parable of the lost son displays this attitude.

The older brother became angry and refused to go in. So his father went out and pleaded with him. But he answered his father, "Look! All these years I've been slaving for you and never disobeyed your orders. Yet you never gave me even a young goat so I could celebrate with my friends. But when this son of yours who has squandered your property with prostitutes comes home, you kill the fattened calf for him!" "My son," the father said, "you are always with me, and everything I have is yours. But we had to celebrate and be glad, because this brother of yours was dead and is alive again; he was lost and is found" (Luke 15:28-32).

Those who haven't seen the need for forgiveness have trouble with God's grace (Luke 7:36-48).

The first indication in Scripture that God had a gracious plan is seen in the shadow of the Garden of Eden during God's conversation with the serpent:

> And I will put enmity
> > between you and the woman,
> > and between your offspring and hers;
> he will crush your head,
> > and you will strike his heel (Genesis 3:15).

This Scripture isn't directly quoted in the New Testament as pertaining to Jesus, but it is usually considered as such by biblical scholars.

The first clear reference to God's vision for the world is found in His selecting Abraham as the one through whom the world would be blessed.

Introduction

The L<small>ORD</small> had said to Abram, "Leave your country, your people and your father's household and go to the land I will show you.

> I will make you into a great nation,
>   and I will bless you;
> I will make your name great,
>   and you will be a blessing.
> I will bless those who bless you,
>   and whoever curses you I will curse;
> and all peoples on earth
>   will be blessed through you" (Genesis 12:1-3).

Later, when Abraham trusted God to the extent that he was willing to offer Isaac as a sacrifice, God renewed the promise.

The angel of the L<small>ORD</small> called to Abraham from heaven a second time and said, "I swear by myself, declares the L<small>ORD</small>, that because you have done this and have not withheld your son, your only son, I will surely bless you and make your descendants as numerous as the stars in the sky and as the sand on the seashore. Your descendants will take possession of the cities of their enemies, and through your offspring all nations on earth will be blessed, because you have obeyed me" (Genesis 22:15-18).

Abraham didn't fully understand how all nations would be blessed, but Peter accurately explained it to the Jews years later.

Indeed, all the prophets from Samuel on, as many as have spoken, have foretold these days. And you are heirs of the prophets and of the covenant God made with your fathers. He said to Abraham, "Through your offspring all peoples on earth will be blessed." When God raised up his servant, he sent him first to you to bless you by turning each of you from your wicked ways (Acts 3:24-26).

Paul used these same verses to explain to the Galatians the meaning of the Abrahamic promise: "The Scripture foresaw that God would justify the Gentiles by faith, and announced the gospel in advance to Abraham: 'All nations will be blessed through you' " (Galatians 3:8). Beginning with Abraham, God's intentions were clear—to save all nations! Isaiah reinforced this belief when he foresaw a day when all the nations would be a part of God's kingdom.

> This is what Isaiah son of Amoz saw
> concerning Judah and Jerusalem:
> In the last days
> the mountain of the LORD's temple will be established
>   as chief among the mountains;
> it will be raised above the hills,
>   and all nations will stream to it.
> Many peoples will come and say,
> "Come, let us go up to the mountain of the LORD,
>   to the house of the God of Jacob.
> He will teach us his ways,
>   so that we may walk in his paths."
> The law will go out from Zion,
>   the word of the LORD from Jerusalem.
> He will judge between the nations
>   and will settle disputes for many peoples.
> They will beat their swords into plowshares
>   and their spears into pruning hooks.
> Nation will not take up sword against nation,
>   nor will they train for war anymore (Isaiah 2:1-4).

God's gracious intent to save is seen in the inspired writings of the New Testament: "This is good, and pleases God our Savior, who wants all men to be saved and to come to a knowledge of the truth" (1 Timothy 2:3-4); "The Lord is not slow in keeping his promise, as some understand slowness. He is patient with you, not wanting anyone to perish, but everyone to come to repentance" (2 Peter 3:9). Filled with the intent to save His crowning act of creation (Genesis 1:26), God schemed a plan whereby man could be saved. The church is a part of that eternal plan and purpose. Paul wrote, "His intent was that now, through the church, the manifold wisdom of God should be made known to the rulers and authorities in the heavenly realms, according to his eternal purpose which he accomplished in Christ Jesus our Lord" (Ephesians 3:10-11).

God's grace is essential to the plan for saving the world. God knew of man's inclination to disobey and to try to justify himself by works (Luke 18:9-14). Man has been, and always will be, saved by grace. The law was given to break man's pride and to get him to seek God. "What, then, was the purpose of the law? It was added because of transgressions until the Seed to whom the promise referred had come. The law was put into effect through angels by a mediator" (Galatians 3:19). The book of Galatians is a beautiful revelation of all parts of God's vision for man.

The message of Galatians is this: what we are should be viewed as God's gift to us, and what we finally become (Galatians 4:19) is our gift to God.

CONTENTS

CHAPTER ONE

HOW MAN IS SAVED

Introduction

The impact of this relatively short book of Galatians on religion is immeasurable. Romans and Galatians have been study guides for Protestantism since the sixteenth century. Galatians reflects the first major crisis in the early church. But there was more at stake than a small group of churches in south Galatia—the success or failure of missionary activity in the Roman world (and in subsequent worlds) was involved. The issue wasn't how much Judaism Gentiles could be expected to embrace, but whether or not the gospel was sufficient to save apart from human efforts.

There is some question about the recipients of the letter. Arguments abound for the geographical area known as Galatia as opposed to the political province with the same name. However, the evidence tends to be more supportive of the view that these were churches in Asia Minor located in the Roman province of Galatia. In keeping with this view, then, the towns mentioned in Acts 13, 14, and 16:1-5 (Pisidian Antioch, Iconium, Lystra, and Derbe) are the ones that received the letter. Galatians was probably written in A.D. 47 or 48 prior to Paul's second missionary journey.

1

When the gospel is introduced into any culture, ideas associated with that culture sometimes hinder its acceptance. The Greeks emphasized learning and knowledge. Because of their great confidence in human wisdom, it was difficult for them to accept the message of the cross.

For the message of the cross is foolishness to those who are perishing, but to us who are being saved it is the power of God. . . . For since in the wisdom of God the world through its wisdom did not know him, God was pleased through the foolishness of what was preached to save those who believe. Jews demand miraculous signs and Greeks look for wisdom, but we preach Christ crucified: a stumbling block to Jews and foolishness to Gentiles, but to those whom God has called, both Jews and Greeks, Christ the power of God and the wisdom of God (1 Corinthians 1:18, 21-24).

In the Jewish culture, the Jews saw the law as grounds for justification and as a necessary element in the process of justification.

What then shall we say? That the Gentiles, who did not pursue righteousness, have obtained it, a righteousness that is by faith; but Israel, who pursued a law of righteousness, has not attained it. Why not? Because they pursued it not by faith but as if it were by works. They stumbled over the "stumbling stone" (Romans 9:30-32).

The challenge of the gospel was to find acceptance in all cultures.

Theme

In some of the New Testament books, a key verse reflects the content. For example, the thrust of the first eight chapters of Romans is summed up in Romans 1:17 when Paul declared, "The righteous will live by faith."

Acts is summarized in Acts 1:8: "But you will receive power when the Holy Spirit comes on you; and you will be my witnesses in Jerusalem, and in all Judea and Samaria, and to the ends of the earth." This verse gives the geographical outline of the book: chapters 1–7, Jerusalem and Judea; chapters 8–12, Samaria and surrounding areas; chapters 13–28, all the world.

It isn't easy to find the key verse in Galatians, but probably the best choice is found in chapter 2: "We who are Jews by birth and not 'Gentile sinners' know that a man is not justified by observing the law, but by faith in Jesus Christ. So we, too, have put our faith in Christ Jesus that we may be justified by faith in Christ and not by observing the law, because by observing the law no one will be justified" (verses 15-16).

These verses are found in context with Paul's rebuke of Peter. It isn't clear if this is a part of the rebuke or merely Paul's elaboration of the rebuke, but in either case the verses serve as the theme statement for the major thrust of the book—how man is saved.

Verse 16 appears to be given in three stages. Stage one is a general statement—"A man is not justified by observing the law." Stage two is a statement that included Paul, Peter, and the Galatians—"We may be justified by faith in Christ and not by observing the law." Stage three is a universal statement—"By observing the law no one ["no flesh," NASV] will be justified." Verse 15 stated a relationship by birth, but in verse 16, Paul said, "We know," which means knowledge by conviction.

Verse 16 also contains several firsts for the book. It is the first time that justification, and law, are mentioned and the first time faith is mentioned as a channel of salvation. *Justification* means "to declare righteous or innocent"; it is the opposite of condemnation or of being pronounced guilty. Justification is the act of God—without any help from man—pardoning the guilty. However, when you have been justified, you are not only rendered guiltless; you are also reinstated as an heir and as a child. "If you belong to Christ, then you are Abraham's seed, and *heirs* according to the promise" (Galatians 3:29, emphasis added). "So you are no longer a slave, but a *son;* and since you are a *son,* God has made you also an *heir*" (Galatians 4:7, emphasis added).

Paul's attack on the law of Moses as being a system based on human merit that purports salvation isn't limited to only the Mosaical law system but includes any man-made law-keeping system promising a relationship with, or approval by, God. Paul's polemic against the law of Moses is broad enough to include any law system—past, present, or future. The law of Moses is purely an example of the principles that Paul was challenging.

It's important to understand the purposes behind the law of Moses.

1. The law made man conscious of sin. "Therefore no one will be declared righteous in his sight by observing the law; rather, through the law we become conscious of sin" (Romans 3:20). It's possible to sin without knowing it, but law makes you aware of it.

2. The law exposed transgressions. "And where there is no law there is no transgression" (Romans 4:15b). "But sin is not taken into account when there is no law" (Romans 5:13b).

3. The law assisted man in recognizing sin. "Did that which is good, then, become death to me? By no means! But in order that sin might be recognized as

4

sin, it produced death in me through what was good, so that through the commandment sin might become utterly sinful" (Romans 7:13).

4. The law was added (to the promise of Abraham) to reveal or expose transgressions until Jesus comes. "What, then, was the purpose of the law? It was added because of transgressions until the Seed to whom the promise referred had come" (Galatians 3:19a).

5. The law led man to Christ so he could be justified. "So the law was put in charge to lead us to Christ that we might be justified by faith" (Galatians 3:24).

It is increasingly clear that the law—any law—doesn't justify. In fact, the law did just the opposite in that it aroused fleshly desires and passions. Man is filled with curiosity and a desire to experiment. Armed with the curiosity to learn by doing or experiencing, man is drawn to the forbidden. What do you do when you see a sign that says, "Wet Paint: Do Not Touch"? Do you touch? Or what about the one that says, "Don't Look on the Other Side of This Sign"? Do you look? The law can't justify, but it can lead you to the One who can—Jesus! The law wasn't all bad (Romans 7:12), but it was never meant to be the power to energize the man of God. The law served as a map to lead man to God and to show him the need for dependence on God.

The Pharisees, a Jewish sect, led the opposition against Paul's belief that salvation is by grace. They didn't view the law as being optional for Christians; they considered it a necessary addition to the gospel. "Some men came down from Judea to Antioch and were teaching the brothers: *'Unless* you are circumcised, according to the custom taught by Moses, *you cannot be saved.'* . . . Now then, why do you try to test God by putting on the necks of the disciples a yoke that neither we nor our fathers have been able to bear?"

(Acts 15:1, 10, emphasis added). The Pharisees' view was in direct opposition to the book of Galatians and to the gospel that Paul preached. "Through him everyone who believes is justified from everything you could not be justified from by the law of Moses" (Acts 13:39).

Faith is mentioned three times in Galatians 2:16, which emphasizes its importance. Faith is trust that starts with a knowledge of facts. It involves a personal trust in Jesus and is the means to the source of justification. Paul stressed Jesus as the object of trust when he visited the Galatians on his first journey. "Paul and Barnabas appointed elders for them in each church and, with prayer and fasting, committed them to the Lord in whom they had put their trust" (Acts 14:23).

Man's own righteousness is one of the major obstacles to justification. Paul maintained that this was the reason the Israelites missed salvation: "Brothers, my heart's desire and prayer to God for the Israelites is that they may be saved. For I can testify about them that they are zealous for God, but their zeal is not based on knowledge. Since they did not know the righteousness that comes from God and sought to establish their own, they did not submit to God's righteousness" (Romans 10:1-3). As a Pharisee, Paul knew the temptation for man to trust in his own righteousness. He knew that he needed a righteousness from God: "Not having a righteousness of my own that comes from the law, but that which is through faith in Christ—the righteousness that comes from God and is by faith" (Philippians 3:9).

Personal righteousness as a hindrance to a relationship with God is seen in one of Jesus' parables. The setting for this parable was established by these words: "To some who were confident of their own righteousness and looked down on everybody else, Jesus told this parable" (Luke 18:9). As a result of their own righteousness, they looked down on others. With this explanation, the parable is given.

Two men went up to the temple to pray, one a Pharisee and the other a tax collector. The Pharisee stood up and prayed about himself: "God, I thank you that I am not like all other men—robbers, evildoers, adulterers—or even like this tax collector. I fast twice a week and give a tenth of all I get." But the tax collector stood at a distance. He would not even look up to heaven, but beat his breast and said, "God, have mercy on me, a sinner." I tell you that this man, rather than the other, went home justified before God. For everyone who exalts himself will be humbled, and he who humbles himself will be exalted (Luke 18:10-14).

The Pharisee placed his trust in *his* actions as proof of God's approval. The book of Galatians stands as a bulwark against self-help salvation and man-made religion.

Another example of depending on one's righteous acts as a basis for salvation is seen in Jesus' encounter with the rich young man. "Now a man came up to Jesus and asked, 'Teacher, what good thing must I do to get eternal life?'" (Matthew 19:16). Note the attitude expressed in his request—"What good thing must I do?" He later admitted to being obedient to those commandments that he could do. There was nothing wrong in his *doing*, except for the fact that he felt he would receive in proportion to what he had *done*. Man's actions will never cause God to be indebted to him.

The Galatian letter is extremely personal and human. At various points Paul was surprised (1:6), blunt (3:1), pleading (4:12), passionate (4:19-20), sarcastic (5:12), and bold (6:17). It has three major divisions.

The first one is personal (chapters 1–2); we discover who Paul is. The second is doctrinal (chapters 3–4); we learn about what Paul taught. And the third division is practical (chapters 5–6); we see how to apply what he taught.

Thought Questions for Chapter One

1. Give some one-word descriptions of God.
2. How would you describe today's culture? How does it differ from that of Paul's day?
3. In what do some individuals trust for their justification?
4. Why do some people believe they must earn what they receive?
5. Is the Pharisee's attitude evident today? (Luke 18:9-14) In whom?

CHAPTER
TWO

JUSTIFICATION AND
THE DEATH OF CHRIST

Justification (being made guiltless) and its relationship to the death of Christ is thematic throughout the Bible. Covering all the doctrinal teachings on atonement (Christ's suffering and death on the cross, reconciling man to God) extends beyond the bounds of this book's central topic. However, Galatians presupposes a knowledge of the atonement of Jesus, so some basic points about the subject must be considered.

A discussion on the sacrifice of Jesus must begin with the prediction of His death in Isaiah 53. The purpose for Jesus' suffering was for man's justification.

> After the suffering of his soul,
>   he will see the light of life and be satisfied;
> by his knowledge my righteous
>   servant will justify many,
>   and he will bear their iniquities (Isaiah 53:11).

Isaiah 53 also teaches the substitutional atonement of Jesus. The background for understanding this type of atonement is rooted in the Old Testament system of sacrifices.

When Aaron has finished making atonement for the Most Holy Place, the Tent of Meeting and the altar, he shall bring forward the live goat. He is to lay both hands on the head of the live goat and confess over it all the wickedness and rebellion of the Israelites—all their sins—and put them on the goat's head. He shall send the goat away into the desert in the care of a man appointed for the task. The goat will carry on itself all their sins to a solitary place; and the man shall release it in the desert (Leviticus 16:20-22).

In Isaiah 53, Jesus is likened to a lamb being led to slaughter (verse 7). The wayward man is likened to a sheep gone astray who needs help. The solution to straying sheep was the offering of Jesus.

> We all, like sheep, have gone astray,
>   each of us has turned to his own way;
> and the LORD has laid on him
>   the iniquity of us all (Isaiah 53:6).

The "laid on him" action corresponds to Aaron's laying his hands on the goat (Leviticus 16:21).

Man is made righteous by the death of Jesus. Jesus willingly became sin for us (He became a curse for us [Galatians 3:13]) in order to supply the means (in Him) by which we become righteous. "God made him who had no sin to be sin for us, so that in him we might become the righteousness of God" (2 Corinthians 5:21). Peter gave additional insight by connecting the death of Jesus and the righteousness that man needs: "He himself bore our sins in his body on the tree, so that we might die to sin and live for righteousness; by his wounds you have been healed" (1 Peter 2:24); "Christ died for sins once for all, the righteous for the unrighteous, to bring you to God" (1 Peter 3:18a).

Paul put the major elements of justification in one compact section.

But now a righteousness from God, apart from law, has been made known, to which the Law and the Prophets testify. This righteousness from God comes through faith in Jesus Christ to all who believe. There is no difference, for all have sinned and fall short of the glory of God, and are justified freely by his grace through the redemption that came by Christ Jesus (Romans 3:21-24).

His central message in Galatians is that righteousness from God is possible apart from law and comes only through faith in Jesus Christ. Justification is by Jesus' grace. In this passage from Romans "justified" is passive, which means man received the action. Man was "justified freely," which means without cause or cost. The root word for "freely" means "gift." This same word is used in John 15:25—"they hated me without reason"—meaning "without cause." Man is righteous without causing it and receives a forgiveness he didn't pay for.

Because God's basic nature is holy (Exodus 3:5; Psalm 111:9; Hebrews 12:14; 1 Peter 1:16), sin insults Him and results in His anger and wrath. Jesus becomes the "sacrifice of atonement": "God presented him as a sacrifice of atonement, through faith in his blood. He did this to demonstrate his justice, because in his forbearance he had left the sins committed beforehand unpunished" (Romans 3:25). The meaning of "sacrifice of atonement" ("propitiation," NASV) can be traced to the Old Testament where the mercy seat was the place of atonement (Hebrews 9:5). In the New Testament, the mercy seat was replaced by Christ on the cross. Christ's sacrifice appeased the wrath of God (Romans 1:18; Ephesians 5:6) and satisfied God's justice because sin was punished at the cross.

Surely he took up our infirmities
    and carried our sorrows,
yet we considered him stricken by God,
    smitten by him, and afflicted.
But he was pierced for our transgressions,
    he was crushed for our iniquities;
the punishment that brought us peace was upon him,
    and by his wounds we are healed (Isaiah 53:4-5).

Faith in Jesus allows God to justify all men. "He did it to demonstrate his justice at the present time, so as to be just and the one who justifies those who have faith in Jesus" (Romans 3:26). Man's justification by faith doesn't allow him to boast, though. "Where, then, is boasting? It is excluded. On what principle? On that of observing the law? No, but on that of faith. For we maintain that a man is justified by faith apart from observing the law" (Romans 3:27-28). All men are justified on the same basis—faith in Christ—whether Jew or Gentile. "Is God the God of Jews only? Is he not the God of Gentiles too? Yes, of Gentiles, too, since there is only one God, who will justify the circumcised by faith and the uncircumcised through that same faith" (Romans 3:29-30).

As Paul explained the cross to those who trusted in their own wisdom, he also declared that Jesus is the wisdom of God, "our righteousness, holiness and redemption" (1 Corinthians 1:30). In the death of Jesus, man's sins were given to Him (Isaiah 53:4-6), and His righteousness was given to man. With man clothed in Christ's righteousness, God can save him because of his position and relationship with Him through His Son. Man isn't to boast because of his meritorious acts of obedience, but he boasts because of his exalted position in the Lord: "Therefore, as it is written: 'Let him who boasts boast in the Lord' " (1 Corinthians 1:31).

With the doctrine of atonement clearly engrained in his mind, Paul felt man had nothing to boast about except in the cross. The contrast between Paul's boasting and his opponents' boasting in Galatians is the difference in understanding how man is saved. "Not even those who are circumcised obey the law, yet they want you to be circumcised that they may boast about your flesh. May I never boast except in the cross of our Lord Jesus Christ, through which the world has been crucified to me, and I to the world" (Galatians 6:13-14).

The death of Jesus is connected with baptism. Paul taught the necessity of one's dying to be "freed from sin" (Romans 6:7). At the beginning of Romans 6, Paul used "into" three times: "Or don't you know that all of us who were baptized *into* Christ Jesus were baptized *into* his death? We were therefore buried with him through baptism *into* death in order that, just as Christ was raised from the dead through the glory of the Father, we too may live a new life" (Romans 6:3-4, emphasis added). Paul stated that baptism is *into* the death of Christ and *into* the "benefits" of His death. One of those benefits is reconciliation (being brought into a harmonious relationship with God; made right). "For if, when we were God's enemies, we were reconciled to him through the death of his Son, how much more, having been reconciled, shall we be saved through his life!" (Romans 5:10). Baptism unites man with Jesus and the benefits of His death. However, baptism also becomes the place of his death (Romans 6:4), resulting in his freedom from sin (Romans 6:7). Baptism becomes both a tomb and a womb.

The death of the only Son of God (John 3:16) is positive proof of God's generous nature. The book of

Galatians reveals a God who wants to save more than He wants to condemn. The world has more difficulty accepting a God who saves by grace than it does accepting a God who demands perfect obedience to a law-keeping system. Most people feel that God is more interested in condemnation than salvation. They see God as a "cosmic Santa Claus" who is making His list and checking it twice to punish the naughty and reward the nice! There are only two means for justification: grace or law. Since man's compliance with the demands of the law isn't practical, grace is his only hope.

The death of Jesus shows man's total inadequacy to save himself. Man is saved by the work of God at the cross, not by his biblical skills or perfect worship (even though biblical skills and correct worship are important). "Nothing in my hand I bring, simply to the cross I cling" must be more than words in a songbook; they must be the belief of every Christian!

Thought Questions for Chapter Two

1. If justification is important, why are some people not interested in the subject?
2. What does Isaiah 53 teach us about Jesus?
3. What does the prediction of Christ's death tell us about God?
4. What is the problem between trusting in your faith and trusting in your works?
5. How can one believe he must be baptized, but at the same time not be tempted to trust in himself but in God?

CHAPTER
THREE

PAUL'S FIRST
MISSIONARY
JOURNEY

Paul's conversion from Judaism to Christianity has to be considered one of the major events of the first-century church. His dramatic turnaround was hard for many to believe (Acts 9:13-14, 26). Involved in his conversion was a commission to be a vital force in evangelizing the world—a part of the Abrahamic promise. The Lord's response to a reluctant Ananias made Paul's future clear. "But the Lord said to Ananias, 'Go! This man is my chosen instrument to carry my name before the Gentiles and their kings and before the people of Israel' " (Acts 9:15).

The church at Antioch of Syria was a logical place to launch a ministry to the Gentiles since this church was more Greek than Jewish.

Now those who had been scattered by the persecution in connection with Stephen traveled as far as Phoenicia, Cyprus and Antioch, telling the message only to Jews. Some of them, however, men from Cyprus and Cyrene, went to Antioch and began to speak to Greeks also, telling them the good news about the Lord Jesus. The Lord's hand was with them, and a great number of people believed and turned to the Lord (Acts 11:19-21).

Accompanied by Barnabas and John Mark, Paul sailed for Cyprus (Acts 13:4). Their trip brought them to Antioch of Pisidia, and they went immediately to the synagogue (Acts 13:14). When Paul was given permission to speak, he addressed the audience, "Men of Israel and you Gentiles who worship God, listen to me!" (Acts 13:16). Later in the sermon, he addressed them as "brothers, children of Abraham, and you God-fearing Gentiles" (Acts 13:26). When he returned on the following Sabbath, he was treated harshly and thus announced, "We had to speak the word of God to you first. Since you reject it and do not consider yourselves worthy of eternal life, we now turn to the Gentiles" (Acts 13:46). In support of this judgment and radical action, Paul quoted Isaiah 49:6 as recorded in Acts 13:47: "For this is what the Lord has commanded us: 'I have made you a light for the Gentiles, that you may bring salvation to the ends of the earth.' "

This encounter at the synagogue and subsequent events raise some questions. (1) Why were Gentiles at a Jewish synagogue? (2) If Paul was already preaching to Gentiles, how could he *now* turn to Gentiles? The biblical student needs to be aware of four classes of people to whom the gospel was preached. The first class included Jews or Hebrews (men of Israel or children of Abraham [Acts 13:16, 26]) who worshiped God according to the law of Moses.

The second class consisted of Gentile proselytes who had become full-fledged members of Israel. It isn't known how much evangelism the Jews did, but their efforts didn't escape Jesus' notice (Matthew 23:15). These proselytes were referred to as "devout converts to Judaism" (Acts 13:43).

The third class was made up of Gentiles who worshiped God and were known as God-fearers (Acts 13:16, 26, 50; 17:17). These Gentiles rejected pagan gods and embraced the God of the Jews but didn't accept the religion of the Jews. They weren't considered members of Israel, but their life-styles were harmonious with Jewish morals. The most famous representative of this class is Cornelius, who is described as being a God-fearing believer and extremely moral. "He and all his family were devout and God-fearing; he gave generously to those in need and prayed to God regularly" (Acts 10:2); "The men replied, 'We have come from Cornelius the centurion. He is a righteous and God-fearing man, who is respected by all the Jewish people" (Acts 10:22). These Gentiles were very well acquainted with Jewish ways and literature.

In the fourth class were pagan, polytheistic Gentiles. Paul turned to this group in Acts 13:46. These people were famous for their perverted life-style and practice of life-dominating sins (1 Corinthians 5:1; 6:9-11). Their polytheistic beliefs (more than one god) were apparent when Paul reached Lystra.

When the crowd saw what Paul had done, they shouted in the Lycaonian language, "The gods have come down to us in human form!" Barnabas they called Zeus, and Paul they called Hermes because he was the chief speaker. The priest of Zeus, whose temple was just outside the city, brought bulls and wreaths to the city gates because he and the crowd wanted to offer sacrifices to them (Acts 14:11-13).

It was from these four classes of people that the churches were formed in the region of southern Galatia. Disciples were left in every town where Paul preached in this region. "They preached the good news in that city [Derbe] and won a large number of disciples. Then they returned to Lystra, Iconium and Antioch, strengthening the disciples and encouraging them to remain true to the faith. 'We must go through many hardships to enter the kingdom of God,' they said" (Acts 14:21-22).

The two sermons that Paul preached at Antioch and Lystra demonstrated his message. In Galatians 1:6-9, he spoke of the gospel he had preached to the people there. The sermon at Antioch begins with a summary of Old Testament history that was familiar to all the listeners in the synagogue.

The God of the people of Israel chose our fathers; he made the people prosper during their stay in Egypt, with mighty power he led them out of that country, he endured their conduct for about forty years in the desert, he overthrew seven nations in Canaan and gave their land to his people as their inheritance. All this took about 450 years. After this, God gave them judges until the time of Samuel the prophet. Then the people asked for a king, and he gave them Saul son of Kish, of the tribe of Benjamin, who ruled forty years. After removing Saul, he made David their king. He testified concerning him: "I have found David son of Jesse a man after my own heart; he will do everything I want him to do" (Acts 13:17-22).

With the audience in agreement with his view of Old Testament events, Paul moved into the heart of his message—Jesus. He introduced the ministry of Jesus in the context of John the Baptist's work and connected it with King David.

From this man's descendants God has brought to Israel the Savior Jesus, as he promised. Before the coming of Jesus, John preached repentance and baptism to all the people of Israel. As John was completing his work, he said: "Who do you think I am? I am not that one. No, but he is coming after me, whose sandals I am not worthy to untie." Brothers, children of Abraham, and you God-fearing Gentiles, it is to us that this message of salvation has been sent (Acts 13:23-26).

Paul declared the innocent nature of Jesus and the failure of the Jews to see how He had fulfilled the prophets' predictions.

The people of Jerusalem and their rulers did not recognize Jesus, yet in condemning him they fulfilled the words of the prophets that are read every Sabbath. Though they found no proper ground for a death sentence, they asked Pilate to have him executed. When they had carried out all that was written about him, they took him down from the tree and laid him in a tomb (Acts 13:27-29).

Paul alluded to the preaching of Jesus and Him crucified in Galatians 3:1 (see 1 Corinthians 2:2). At the heart of Jesus' message is the good news of His resurrection, which can be proved by witnesses and by the affirmations of Old Testament Scripture.

But God raised him from the dead, and for many days he was seen by those who had traveled with him from Galilee to Jerusalem. They are now his witnesses to our people. We tell you the good news: What God promised our fathers he has fulfilled for us, their children, by raising up Jesus. As it is written in the second Psalm: "You are my Son; today I have become your Father." The fact that God raised him from the dead, never to decay, is stated in these words: "I will give you the holy and sure blessings promised to David." So it is stated elsewhere: "You will not let your Holy One see decay." For when David had served God's purpose in his own generation, he fell asleep; he was buried with his fathers and his body decayed. But the one whom God raised from the dead did not see decay (Acts 13:30-37).

The good news is made better because forgiveness of sins and justification are now possible. This could never be true of the previous law-keeping system. "Therefore, my brothers, I want you to know that through Jesus the forgiveness of sins is proclaimed to you. Through him everyone who believes is justified from everything you could not be justified from by the law of Moses" (Acts 13:38-39). Paul ended his sermon with a solemn warning about rejecting the gospel of good news:

Take care that what the prophets have said does not happen to you:
> "Look, you scoffers,
> wonder and perish,
> for I am going to do something in your days
> that you would never believe,
> even if someone told you" (Acts 13:40-41).

The response to the sermon appeared to be good because Paul was invited to return the next Sabbath. Even after the formal meeting was over, conversation continued between Paul and his listeners. These conversations centered on the grace of God (Galatians 1:6; 2:21; 3:18; 5:4; 6:18). "As Paul and Barnabas were leaving the synagogue, the people invited them to speak further about these things on the next Sabbath. When the congregation was dismissed, many of the Jews and devout converts to Judaism followed Paul and Barnabas, who talked with them and urged them to continue in the *grace of God*" (Acts 13:42-43, emphasis added).

However, on the next Sabbath, Paul and Barnabas's reception was quite different because the Jews didn't like the popularity that this new message was receiving. "On the next Sabbath almost the whole city gathered to hear the word of the Lord. When the Jews saw the crowds, they were filled with jealousy and talked abusively against what Paul was saying" (Acts 13:44-45).

Paul used a different approach in his message at Lystra because he was speaking to people who did not have an Old Testament background. Barnabas and Paul had to convince them that they (Paul and Barnabas) weren't gods and shouldn't receive sacrifices (Acts 14:13-15). Paul began by declaring "good news":

We are bringing you good news, telling you to turn from these worthless things to the living God, who made heaven and earth and sea and everything in them. In the past, he let all nations go their own way. Yet he has not left himself without testimony: He has shown kindness by giving you rain from heaven and crops in their seasons; he provides you with plenty of food and fills your hearts with joy (Acts 14:15-17).

Paul's argument for God was based not on Old Testament Scripture but on natural revelation through creation (Acts 17:24; Romans 1:20). The opposition that occurred in Antioch and Iconium followed Paul and Barnabas to Lystra. It's noteworthy to observe that the people who had insisted that Paul and Barnabas were gods and should receive sacrifices (Acts 14:11-15, 18) were the same ones who participated in Paul's stoning. *Fickle* could aptly describe such people and explain how they changed so quickly from one gospel to a different one (Galatians 1:6-9).

Paul's next stop on the first journey was Derbe. "They preached *good news* in that city and won a large number of disciples" (Acts 14:21a, emphasis added). When Paul and Barnabas returned to these towns on their way to Antioch (Syria), they urged "them to remain true to the faith" (Acts 14:22). "Faith" here is synonymous with the gospel (see Acts 6:7; 13:8;

Galatians 1:23; Jude 3, 20). Paul and Barnabas committed these young converts "to the Lord, *in whom they had put their trust*" (Acts 14:23, emphasis added). Stopping off in Perga, they "preached the word" (Acts 14:25). "Preaching the word" is the same as "preaching the cross as the power of God" (1 Corinthians 1:18, NASV). The "word of the Lord" spread wherever it was preached (Acts 13:49).

Acts 13 and 14 provide background information for the book of Galatians and insights into the people who made up the Galatian churches and the message preached to them. Galatians 3 and 4 contain an in-depth look into the nature of the good news.

Thought Questions for Chapter Three

1. Discuss God's part in Paul's conversion.
2. How can the gospel be adapted to meet the needs of the various peoples in our world?
3. What part(s) of the gospel message is the most confusing or the hardest for modern man to accept?
4. What do you think should be emphasized in today's sermons?
5. What has to be true of people before they can accept the gospel?

CHAPTER
FOUR

FALSE TEACHERS
ARRIVE IN GALATIA

Acts 13 and 14 present a view of the first missionary efforts among pagans who, for the most part, didn't have a background similar to the Jews and the God-fearing Gentiles. The conflict between Paul and the false brothers (Galatians 2:4) was caused by a clash in missionary methods. Evangelizing this area of the world raised two questions: (1) How do you keep people doing right without law? and (2) How do you encourage proper Christian behavior without destroying Christianity? The gospel of Christ was Paul's answer to these two questions (Galatians 1:7). Grace isn't simply a doctrine; it's a life-style that controls how you live before God. It's a relationship, not a checklist.

The Judaizers (Christian Jews who believed that the law of Moses should be kept by Gentile Christians) determined that law should be used to control behavior and to produce behavioral changes. They felt the Christian's orientation or dynamic came from the law rather than from faith in Christ. Paul called their method a "different gospel" (Galatians 1:6).

The Judaizers' objective—behavioral changes as opposed to internal transformation—determined their method. Their approach to religion for centuries had been one of control—"thou shalt not. . . ." For example, to keep Jews from violating the commandment, "Remember the Sabbath day and keep it holy," the Judaizers built "fences" around the law to restrict violations. A "fence" such as healing on the Sabbath ensured that no one would work on that day. But the "fences" were ends in themselves and became equal with the law (Jesus called them "rules taught by men" [Matthew 15:9]). Behavior modification orchestrated the "gospel" they preached.

Paul believed just the opposite; he felt that the nature and essence of the gospel should control the objective. The objective of the Judaizers determined their method; hence, the end (objective) justified the means (different gospel). Paul's objective was "Christ in you" (Galatians 2:20; 4:19), out of which flowed a life in harmony with that presence.

The Judaizers followed Paul in Galatia and taught a "different gospel." By using the Jerusalem leaders to establish their credibility (Acts 15:24; Galatians 2:12), they tried to undermine Paul's apostleship as a means of discrediting his message. They preached a gospel (death, burial, and resurrection) that *sounded* like the gospel the Galatians had accepted; thus, the Galatians had confidence in their new brothers.

Perhaps, in an effort to please, the Galatians accepted the new twist to Paul's gospel and didn't realize its seriousness or its consequences. The new system of legalistic slavery appealed to the Galatians because they had come out of a slavery to the "basic principles of the world" (Galatians 4:3). The new legalism sounded right and had a good purpose (pleasing God), but the differences were enough to destroy them in the long run.

The teachers' sincerity was evident; after all, they were traveling missionaries! However, the false teachers didn't realize they were false because they weren't wrong on *all* doctrinal points. They knew enough right answers to pass a doctrine test, but the areas where they were wrong made the difference between a true and a false gospel.

Internal evidence in the book of Galatians shows the grave consequences of the Judaizers' work among the churches and offers a glimpse of Paul's opposition. Some of the consequences of their work are cited below.

1. The Christians were thrown into a state of confusion. "Evidently some people are throwing you into confusion" (Galatians 1:7). "The one who is throwing you into confusion will pay the penalty, whoever he may be" (Galatians 5:10). Paul was preaching a gospel of salvation by grace that didn't depend on human merit, and the new brothers were teaching the necessity of human effort in salvation. "Some men came down from Judea to Antioch and were teaching the brothers: 'Unless you are circumcised, according to the custom taught by Moses, you cannot be saved' " (Acts 15:1).

2. The Christians were tempted to discriminate against others. This type of discrimination already had taken place in Antioch because of the Judaizers' teaching (Galatians 2:11-13), and the result would be the same in the Galatian churches, which were composed of Jews, converts to Judaism, God-fearers, and pagan Gentiles.

3. The Christians had become enslaved to a controlled, routine religion. "But now that you know God—or rather are known by God—how is it that you are turning back to those weak and miserable principles? Do you wish to be enslaved by them all over again?" (Galatians 4:9).

4. The Christians had lost the joy that had characterized their acceptance of the gospel. "When the Gentiles

heard this, they were glad and honored the word of the Lord; and all who were appointed for eternal life believed" (Acts 13:48). "What has happened to all your joy? I can testify that, if you could have done so, you would have torn out your eyes and given them to me" (Galatians 4:15). When the Christian loses the joy of his salvation (Psalm 51:12), it is proof that his life is lived (Galatians 5:16, 25) and led (Galatians 5:18) without the Spirit.

5. The Christians were developing a divisive attitude by being taught to shun and avoid those who had taught them the gospel. "Those people are zealous to win you over, but for no good. What they want is to alienate you from us, so that you may be zealous for them" (Galatians 4:17).

6. The Christians were displaying actions completely opposite to the fruit of the Spirit. It was clearly stated that "the fruit of the Spirit is love, joy, peace, patience, kindness, goodness, faithfulness, gentleness and self-control" (Galatians 5:22-23). And warnings to the Christians about their behavior were equally clear: "If you keep on biting and devouring each other, watch out or you will be destroyed by each other" (Galatians 5:15); "Let us not become conceited, provoking and envying each other" (Galatians 5:26).

7. The Christians had accepted a gospel based on external measurements as a guide to spirituality; hence, because of man's prideful tendencies, they were becoming competitive with one another. "Each one should test his own actions. Then he can take pride in himself, without comparing himself to somebody else" (Galatians 6:4). Comparing externals (regardless of how true or impressive they might be) doesn't meet with God's approval. It wasn't the boasting Pharisee, but the humble tax collector who "went home justified before God" (Luke 18:14).

8. The different gospel boasted in the flesh rather than in the cross. "Not even those who are circumcised obey the law, yet they want you to be circumcised that they may boast about your flesh. May I never boast except in the cross of our Lord Jesus Christ, through which the world has been crucified to me, and I to the world" (Galatians 6:13-14).

The problem created by the Judaizers centered on the essential nature of the gospel—did it need any additions in order for it to save men? When you buy a gospel based on meritorious works, you will never have peace. When you view your Christian works as being meritorious, you fall into the same trap as the Galatian Christians with their works of the law.

If the twentieth-century Christian believes that his Christian works have merit, he will be led to despair and depression. He'll never go to sleep believing he has done everything he could do or that he has done it as well as it could have been done. No one lives up to his own daily expectations, much less the expectations he believes God has for him.

Today's temptation isn't to return to the works of the law but to make the "Christian system" legalistic, obviously mistrusting the principle of grace. The Christian will never be good enough to save himself; however, God's kindness will lead him to repentance (Romans 2:4). Man is saved, not because he is good, but because God is good.

Salvation is the gift of God (Ephesians 2:8-9). You can't pay for a gift and have it still remain a gift. When you become a Christian, you receive a box of thank-you notes rather than a premium book. Wouldn't you enjoy life more if you had no car payments? What would your attitude be toward writing the bank a monthly thank-you note as opposed to a check? Your life should be a daily thank-you for what God has done for you.

The gospel of grace isn't cheap! It calls for a quality of life that law could never achieve.

The disciple of Jesus shouldn't be afraid of a life oriented in grace. The topic of grace hasn't been frequently discussed during the restoration movement. When grace has been preached, the message has been either, "You can fall from it!" or a reaction to the false claims of "once saved, always saved."

The purpose of this study is to search the book of Galatians to learn how the Christian is justified and about the life-style he will lead as a free man in Christ. Salvation will be seen not only as taking place at a point in time but also as having a relationship with God. A proper understanding of Galatians will help you to remain faithful to God over the long haul. When you realize what you have in Jesus, the temptations of the world will diminish, and a "cheap gospel" will have no appeal. Many Christians leave the Lord because of a misunderstanding of what they have in Jesus.

Thought Questions for Chapter Four

1. Why do false teachers arise?
2. How would you describe a false teacher?
3. Why do people follow false teachers?
4. Can one be a false teacher and not know it?
5. Why does the message of salvation by grace confuse or disturb people?

CHAPTER
FIVE

INTRODUCTION TO
THE LETTER

When Paul wrote a letter, he usually followed the Greek form, which consisted of four sections: (1) salutation (author, addressee, and greeting); (2) thanksgiving (appreciation for the life of the one being addressed); (3) body (the bulk of the letter containing its purpose); and (4) conclusion (closing). Galatians follows this pattern with one glaring exception—there is no thanksgiving. He obviously found nothing to express appreciation for. (See Philippians 1:3-8 and Colossians 1:3-7 for examples of thanksgiving sections.)

A. Paul Explains His Authority (1:1-5)

1. "Paul, an apostle" (1:1a). The word *apostle* was used by the Greeks to describe a naval expedition that represented Greek interests in foreign service; hence, the term meant "one who was sent forth." Jesus used the term to designate His chosen twelve and to describe His intent for them (Luke 6:13). It specifically referred to the twelve but also generally to people like Barnabas and Jesus (Acts 14:14; Hebrews 3:1).

The qualifications for an apostle were given when one was chosen to take Judas's place. "Therefore it is necessary to choose one of the men who have been with us the whole time the Lord Jesus went in and out among us, beginning from John's baptism to the time when Jesus was taken up from us. For one of these must become a witness with us of his resurrection" (Acts 1:21-22). Because it appeared that Paul didn't meet these qualifications, his opponents were likely to discredit him as an apostle and thus cast a reflection on his preaching. Therefore, Paul began the salutation by establishing himself as a genuine apostle. This credibility was woven through the first two chapters with little jabs seen throughout the book.

Normally, Paul didn't brag about himself but usually projected a sincere humility. "Then he appeared to James, then to all the apostles, and last of all he appeared to me also, as to one abnormally born. *For I am the least of the apostles* and do not even deserve to be called an apostle, because I persecuted the church of God" (1 Corinthians 15:7-9, emphasis added). In a way, Paul felt he had been abnormally born because he had been taken from the womb of Judaism and had become an apostle to the Gentiles. He felt undeserving of his apostleship and considered himself to be the "least" of all the apostles. However, the opposition to his apostleship and his message demanded a strong offense on his part from the very beginning of the letter. His use of prepositions and contrasts served to declare his official position. Paul's apostleship wasn't "from" (*apo*) men nor "by" (*dia*) man; *but* "through" (*dia*) Jesus Christ *and* God the Father. "Men" and "man" stand in contrast to Jesus Christ and God the Father. Therefore, Paul's apostleship was like that of the other apostles—from Jesus and God (see Galatians 1:11-12 for similar material).

Paul, his Roman name, meant "little." *Saul,* his Hebrew name, meant "asked for." He may have been named for the first king of Israel (Saul). As a boy, he probably studied the stories of his namesake. Paul was from the tribe of Benjamin (Philippians 3:5), studied in Jerusalem under Gamaliel (Acts 22:3), was born a Roman citizen (Acts 22:28), and often used this privilege in his ministry (Acts 16:37; 22:25; 25:11-12).

2. Paul declared the resurrection (1:1b). Paul saw Jesus after the resurrection (Acts 26:15-18; 1 Corinthians 15:8), making him an eyewitness to the resurrected Lord. Mentioning the resurrection added credibility to statements surrounding it. Three examples of this include the following:

a) Judgment. "For he has set a day when he will judge the world with justice by the man he has appointed. He has given proof of this to all men by raising him from the dead" (Acts 17:31).

b) Second coming. "For they themselves report what kind of reception you gave us. They tell how you turned to God from idols to serve the living and true God, and to wait for his Son from heaven, whom he raised from the dead—Jesus, who rescues us from the coming wrath" (1 Thessalonians 1:9-10).

c) Jesus as the Son of God. "Regarding his Son, who as to his human nature was a descendant of David, and who through the Spirit of holiness was declared with power to be the Son of God by his resurrection from the dead: Jesus Christ our Lord" (Romans 1:3-4).

God reveals Himself by His actions, in a progressive revelation. God made Himself known as the creator, the director of the Exodus, and the source of the resurrection of Jesus. God is a God of history and also manifests Himself in this manner.

3. "And all the brothers with me" (1:2a). Normally, when Paul wrote a letter, he named the brothers who were with him (see Philippians 1:1; 1 Thessalonians 1:1), but the names were omitted in the Galatian letter. There are three possible reasons for this omission: (1) the Galatian brethren already knew who they were; (2) the Galatian brethren didn't know them, and their names wouldn't add to the Galatians' understanding; or (3) the failure to mention the other brothers placed a greater emphasis on Paul as the primary character.

A good reason for Paul to mention "the brothers" showed that others approved of him as an apostle. These opening verses had to establish Paul's credibility as an apostle.

4. "To the churches in Galatia" (1:2b). Much has been written to explain the nature and content of this phrase. When all the possibilities are weighed, the evidence tends to support the area known as southern Galatia, which included the principal cities of Paul's first missionary journey to this region (Antioch of Pisidia, Iconium, Lystra, and Derbe).

Paul's fervent desire was for all churches to grow and do well. After the Jerusalem conference (Acts 15), he revisited the churches started on his first journey to "see how they are doing" (Acts 15:36). He was concerned with all churches (2 Corinthians 11:28) and cared for them as a mother and a father (1 Thessalonians 2:7, 11).

The salutation doesn't contain any qualifying statements, indicating Paul's deep distress over the Galatians' situation. Ordinarily, at this point in the salutation, Paul added statements such as "sanctified in Christ Jesus and called to be holy" (1 Corinthians 1:2), "saints in Christ Jesus" (Philippians 1:1), or "the holy and faithful brothers" (Colossians 1:2), but in his present mind-set, he couldn't add any of these statements.

5. The greeting (1:3). Grace and peace are blessings from God. Grace is positional (found in Christ), and peace is its by-product. If you don't believe you are saved by grace, you won't have peace. Paul's greeting is typical, but its source (God and Jesus) made it special.

6. Redemptive work of Christ (1:4). One of the book's main issues concerns the significance of Christ's work. Paul set the stage for that work in the salutation. Christ's redemptive work, as described by Paul, can be divided into three parts.

a) Nature. Jesus' sacrifice was voluntary and was for a specific purpose (John 10:15). He was the One offering the sacrifice and also serving as the sacrificial lamb, both the giver and the gift. The sacrifice was for our sins (1 Corinthians 15:3; 2 Corinthians 5:21). God couldn't accept animal sacrifices because they were unworthy, and the sacrifice of man was imperfect. Therefore, the only atoning sacrifice was Jesus.

b) Purpose. The purpose of Christ's redemptive work was to deliver or rescue. *Rescue* means to "pluck it out" (Matthew 5:29; 18:9) or to "lift up out of." It is used in context with divine intervention (see Acts 7:10; 12:11; 23:27 for examples). Jesus rescued us, not from the material world, but from the evil that dominates it. "My prayer is not that you take them out of the world but that you protect them from the evil one" (John 17:15). Paul urged the readers of Romans not to conform to this "age" or "world" (Romans 12:2). Satan's power to win has been taken away.

c) Origin. God's plan wasn't accidental but was in accordance with His will (Matthew 26:39; Acts 2:22-23). Why God had this specific plan has always been questioned. The only possible answer is that He wanted to!

7. Doxology (1:5). Glory is always given to God; it is our unbidden response to Him. Paul vividly indicates in Ephesians 3:20-21 that God is to receive glory and praise: "Now to him who is able to do immeasurably more than all we ask or imagine, according to his power that is at work within us, to him be glory in the church and in Christ Jesus throughout all generations, for ever and ever!" Paul didn't say "to the church be glory"; he said "to him [God] by glory *in the church.*" Glorifying God is the Christian's objective. "Let your light shine before men in such a way that they may see your good works, and glorify your Father who is in heaven" (Matthew 5:16, NASV). "For you have been bought with a price: therefore glorify God in your body" (1 Corinthians 6:20, NASV).

B. Paul and the False Teachers (1:6-10)

Paul revealed his emotional concern where an expression of thanksgiving normally appears in a letter. In this section you can nearly feel Paul's heart throb with anguish.

1. The Galatians' defection (1:6-7a). Paul was astonished at the Galatians' defection; he was "dumbfounded," "blown away." Their defection took place "so quickly," which indicates a short time between their conversion and Paul's writing the letter. "Deserting" is present tense, showing that it was still happening but hadn't reached its final stage. They were AWOL from the One who had called them, God Himself. God's grace had been the means or agent of their calling and is thematic throughout the book (1:3, 6, 15; 2:9, 21; 5:4; 6:18).

The Galatians had accepted a different gospel. Two words for "different" could have been used. One word (*allos*) means "different in the sense of another of the same kind." Your watch can be different from mine, but it is still a watch. A second word for different (*heteros*) means "another of a different kind." Paul used the latter word to mark the contrast between his gospel and the one the Galatians had accepted. That is why Paul quickly added that this different gospel was really no gospel at all.

2. The false teachers' heresy (1:7b-9). "Some people" were Paul's unnamed opponents. In other places, he also chose not to name his opponents (Galatians 2:12; 1 Corinthians 4:18; 2 Corinthians 3:1; 10:2). They were engaged in two activities:

a) Creating confusion. Confusion means physical agitation or mental disturbance. This word is used several times in the New Testament (Matthew 2:3; John 5:7; 14:1; Galatians 5:10).

b) Perverting the gospel. *Pervert* means to "reverse or change to its very opposite." It is used only two other times in the Bible. Acts 2:20 speaks of the sun being turned into darkness, and James 4:9 speaks of laughter turned into mourning. Paul's opponents had reversed the very nature of the gospel. The law from Mount Sinai was a "do and live" religion. After doing or performing, you earned a right to life (Galatians 3:12). The covenant from Mount Calvary is a "live and do" religion. Because you have been given life, you perform or do. You serve because you are saved, not in order to be saved. You win others to God because you have been won. The poet has said,

> I do not work my soul to save
> For this my Lord has done
> But I do work like any slave
> For the love of God's dear Son.

Reversing the covenant of Jesus places the task of salvation on man. It's the difference between being saved by works and being saved by grace. Christ's gospel has His atonement at the heart of it. When you try to rely on a righteousness that is based on performance, you will always see yourself as a failure. However, you can have assurance and confidence in a righteousness that comes from God (Philippians 3:9) and depends on Him.

Distorting the gospel is equal to distorting the grace of Christ. Your Christian life is characterized by grace. Salvation is the gracious gift of God (Ephesians 2:8-9). The opportunity to decide is a gift from God. It is by grace that you live (1 Corinthians 15:10), stand (Romans 5:1-2), are strengthened (2 Timothy 2:1-4), and are allowed to suffer without complaining (2 Corinthians 12:8-10).

Paul viewed his differences with his opponents not as a matter of opinion but as an issue of major consequence. Without any hesitation or qualifying statement, he declared that those who were preaching this different gospel should be eternally condemned. Repeating the condemnation marked the gravity of the situation. The only difference between verses 8 and 9 is a shift from the messenger (we preached) to the recipients (you received). Later Paul was even more graphic in opposing the false teachers (Galatians 5:12).

3. Attack on Paul's integrity (1:10). This verse begins with the Greek word *gar*, which means "yes, indeed" or "certainly," and contains two rhetorical questions: "Am I now trying to win the approval of men, or of God? Or am I trying to please men?" (1:10a). It's true that Paul sought man's approval before his conversion, but becoming a Christian changed everything. There is a possibility that his opponents were perverting his basic philosophy of becoming all things to all men

(1 Corinthians 9:22). He urged circumcision in some cases (Acts 16:1-3) and opposed it in others (Galatians 2:3). The way Paul handled the situations with Timothy and Titus demonstrated his nonconformity with men, incurring their wrath. If pleasing men was still his goal, he would never have become a servant of Christ.

Application for Today

Paul's letter to the Galatians is an example of his follow-up program for new converts. He knew that conversion was not a benediction but a commencement for all Christians.

New Christians should be treated as new babies. Can you imagine a couple placing a newborn in a well-equipped nursery with instructions on the door telling the baby how to care for himself? Many new converts don't receive vital training in the Lord during their early months of growth. Galatians gives an example of some of the needs that Paul attempted to meet in the lives of young Christians. In 1:1-10 he meets the need for correction.

The major thrust of these verses is Paul's concern about the Galatians' accepting "another gospel." He realized that this departure from what he preached would eventually result in their being "alienated from Christ" (5:4). Why do young Christians accept a false gospel? Perhaps simply because it is appealing. The advertising world knows that selling a product is based on appeal. If the advertiser can learn what appeals to the buyer, he can package his product accordingly. The new gospel that the Galatians bought appealed to their desire for human achievement. It is part of the American dream to get what you want the old-fashioned way—by earning it. Paul's gospel declared man's inability to save himself without the grace of God; the new gospel declared salvation as a result of law-keeping.

Do-it-yourself religion appeals to the independent spirit of mankind. Admitting a lack of ability and a dependence on God is not easy for the self-reliant. He is tempted to depend more on self than on God. Promotion should never be allowed to replace proclamation nor gimmicks to replace the gospel.

New Christians might also accept a false gospel because of the persuasiveness of the false teacher. He can have "fine-sounding arguments" (Colossians 2:4) and a doctrine that has "an appearance of wisdom" (Colossians 2:23), but not be what he appears to be. Jesus warned about false prophets in sheep's clothing (Matthew 7:15).

The old saying, "You can't judge a book by its cover," certainly applies. The false teachers in Galatians gave the appearance of sincerity, love, and concern but led the young Christians in a direction opposed to the true teachings of Christ.

New Christians should be taught to investigate a teaching to avoid following a false gospel blindly. It is good to trust the judgment of others, but we should never forfeit our responsibility to search the Scriptures for ourselves (Acts 17:11). Accepting something blindly without asking and searching can lead to disaster. Sometimes Christians are too lazy to check out answers and would rather "go with the flow." We should never settle for harmony at the expense of the purity of the gospel.

Another attraction of false teachers is that they make the gospel promise more than God intended for it to deliver. Promises of good times, financial prosperity, and popularity are not listed by God as direct benefits of the gospel. To the contrary, Paul revisited this area with the message that hardships would be a part of being in the kingdom. "They preached the good news in that city and won a large number of disciples. Then they returned to Lystra, Iconium and Antioch, strengthening the disciples and encouraging them to remain true to the faith. 'We must go through many hardships to enter the kingdom of God,' they said" (Acts 14:21-22).

The care of new Christians should be the concern of all Christians. They need to be rooted in "grace and peace" (1:3) and be focused on the work of Christ at the cross and the will of God, which will result in praise to God. "Grace and peace to you from God our Father and the Lord Jesus Christ, who gave himself for our sins to rescue us from the present evil age, according to the will of our God and Father, to whom be glory for ever and ever. Amen" (1:3-5).

Thought Questions for Chapter Five

1. What methods can be used to nurture new Christians?
2. Paul stressed his qualifications as a spokesman for God. What qualifications should today's spokesmen for God have?
3. What proof do we have of the resurrection of Jesus?
4. Why were the Galatians so quickly led away by the false teachers?
5. How is the gospel perverted today?

CHAPTER
SIX

APOSTLE OF LIBERTY
—PART I

This is the first of three arguments to establish Paul's credibility as an apostle. The false teacher's favorite attack is to discredit his opponent, enabling him to avoid or "cloud" the issues.

A. Apostle by Divine Approval (1:11-24)

It's obvious that Paul's conversion was different but, nonetheless, authentic.

1. The source of his message was divine (1:11-12). "I want you to know, brothers, that the gospel I preached is not something that man made up. I did not receive it from any man, nor was I taught it; rather, I received it by revelation from Jesus Christ."

"I want you to know" is used to introduce a subject of great importance (1 Corinthians 15:1; 2 Corinthians 8:1). "Brothers" introduces this major section dealing with the source of Paul's gospel and appears at the beginning of other major sections: the scriptural basis of Paul's gospel (3:15); plea for understanding (4:12); superiority of being identified with Isaac (4:28); contrast of sonship and slavery (4:31); appeal to reason (5:11); call to freedom (5:13); and exhortation to assist a fallen brother (6:1). Paul used "brothers" because he didn't want the Galatians to feel that he didn't love them because of his criticism of their beliefs and practices.

Four statements explain the source of Paul's message.

a) The gospel is not made up by men. In this instance, "gospel" isn't limited to death, burial, and resurrection since Paul and the Judaizers agreed on these facts, but their differences involved the interpretation and application of the death, burial, and resurrection.

b) I did not receive it from man. Paul used "I" to emphatically stress that he hadn't received the gospel from men. "Receive" normally described how (by rote memory) the Jews' oral tradition had been handed down.

c) I was not taught it. This is similar to Paul's previous statement and enforced the lack of human instruction in his learning process.

d) "I received it by revelation from Jesus Christ." The Greek word *alla* is used to show a definite contrast and is translated "rather" (NIV) or "but" (NASV). The word *alla* is followed by *dia* ("by," NIV; "through," NASV) conveying the idea of "Jesus as the One revealed" or "Jesus was the agent of the revelation." The former idea (Jesus as the One revealed) seems to be in harmony with 1:15-16: "When God, who set me apart from birth and called me by his grace, was pleased to reveal his Son in me." This view stressed the substance of the gospel rather than the means. When did this revelation occur? It depends on how you translate it. "From Jesus" (NIV) means revealed in a broad sense (Arabia, 1:17-18). "Of Jesus" (RSV; NASV) means the content and was a reference to the Damascus road event.

2. His conversion was of God (1:13-24). This section is at the heart of his first argument in establishing his apostleship as authentic. Paul's conversion is described in five stages.

a) Former life (1:13-14). "For you have heard of my previous way of life in Judaism, how intensely I persecuted the church of God and tried to destroy it. I was advancing in Judaism beyond many Jews of my own age and was extremely zealous for the traditions of my fathers."

"Way of life" refers to the whole life and is also used in 1 Peter 1:15 where it is translated "in all you do" (NIV) or "in all your conduct" (RSV). "In Judaism" is in contrast with Christianity; hence, Christianity shouldn't be seen as a form of Judaism. Paul used the term *Judaism* only twice in all his writings (1:13-14).

There were three separate stages of Paul's former life. The first one included his persecution of the church. He described it as intense, meaning "beyond measure and excessive" (Acts 9:13; 26:11). Paul also "tried to destroy" the church, which shows the extent to which he tried to follow his conscience (Acts 9:2; Galatians 1:23).

The second stage was his progress in Judaism. "Advancing" indicates a definite forward direction, as in one who is blazing a trail. When Paul stated that he was "beyond many Jews of [his] own age," he dispelled the idea that he wasn't really knowledgeable about Judaism.

The third stage was his zeal for his fathers' traditions, both oral and written (Matthew 15:6-9). The double use of "my" ("my own age," "my fathers") indicated his awareness of still belonging to the Jewish people.

b) Reversal (1:15-16a). "But when God, who set me apart from birth and called me by his grace, was pleased to reveal his Son in me so that I might preach him among the Gentiles." God is the only force that could reverse a person with Paul's background, and his reversal is directly tied to God. "Set me apart" referred to his special ministry to the Gentiles (Acts 13:2; Romans 1:1). "From birth" indicated that divine forces had been at work for a long time (Isaiah 44:2; 49:1, 5; Jeremiah 1:4-5). He was called by God's grace, and God was pleased to reveal His Son to Paul. Later, Paul, in turn, revealed Christ to all men (Acts 9:15; 22:15; 26:16-18).

c) Reflection (1:16b-17). "I did not consult any man, nor did I go up to Jerusalem to see those who were apostles before I was, but I went immediately into Arabia and later returned to Damascus." Paul didn't consult with any man ("flesh and blood," NASV; see Matthew 16:19). The word *consult* is used twice (1:17 and 2:6) in Galatians and means "to hold conference with" or "to communicate with someone," thus gaining information by communicating with others.

The statement about his not going to Jerusalem to see those who were apostles before he was showed that Paul's apostleship was equal to theirs. He told his readers of his trip into Arabia, the Nabatean kingdom where Aretas IV ruled (2 Corinthians 11:32). This time period is placed between Acts 9:22 and 9:23. "Three years" (1:18) refers to his time in Arabia and his second stay in Damascus. The point of this section is his lack of contact with the Jerusalem leaders, indicating his message wasn't secondhand or handed down from them to him.

d) Sharing (1:18-20). "Then after three years, I went up to Jerusalem to get acquainted with Peter and stayed with him fifteen days. I saw none of the other apostles—only James, the Lord's brother. I assure you before God that what I am writing you is no lie." Paul used *epeita* (translated as "then" in 1:18 and "later" in 1:21 and 2:1) to introduce three different events: his introduction to the Jerusalem church (1:18); his departure for the ministry (1:21); and his return to Jerusalem with Barnabas (2:1).

The purpose of the Jerusalem visit was to become better acquainted with Peter. "Acquainted" refers to the gathering of information and involves more than talking about personal matters. His visit lasted fifteen days, and during this time, he "moved about freely" (Acts 9:28). The only other apostle he saw was James.

In verse 20, Paul strongly affirmed the truth of his statements. Such affirmations are also found in his other letters (2 Corinthians 1:23; 11:31; 1 Thessalonians 2:5).

e) Telling (1:21-24). "Later I went to Syria and Cilicia. I was personally unknown to the churches of Judea that are in Christ. They only heard the report: 'The man who formerly persecuted us is now preaching the faith he once tried to destroy.' And they praised God because of me." When Paul visited the churches in Judea (Acts 9:30; 11:25), they knew him only by reputation. However, they praised God because of him. They didn't praise the law, nor did they praise Paul because of God. It is God that man should praise (1:5).

In summary, Paul should be considered an apostle with full authority for the following reasons: his message and conversion were from God, and his own record and approval by other Christians proved those things. This section emphasized Paul's independence from the Jerusalem apostles, confirming that his message wasn't handed down to him from men.

Application for Today

This section begins Paul's first major argument to establish his credibility as a teacher from God—his conversion was of God. Paul's conversion was to be one of the most dramatic and unbelievable of all time. No one in the early church would have entertained the remotest possibility that one so radical could ever be convinced to be a follower of Jesus. Paul's conversion teaches us many needed lessons about evangelism.

Everyone Is a Prospect

It was a shock to Ananias's system when the Lord appeared to him and told him to go to Paul.

The Lord told him, "Go to the house of Judas on Straight Street and ask for a man from Tarsus named Saul, for he is praying. In a vision he has seen a man named Ananias come and place his hands on him to restore his sight." "Lord," Ananias answered, "I have heard many reports about this man and all the harm he has done to your saints in Jerusalem. And he has come here with authority from the chief priests to arrest all who call on your name." But the Lord said to Ananias, "Go! This man is my chosen instrument to carry my name before the Gentiles and their kings and before the people of Israel. I will show him how much he must suffer for my name" (Acts 9:11-16).

There are groups of people that seem to intimidate us as soul-winners. Often we don't reach out to the elderly because we assume they are set in their ways, too old to learn, or too rigid in mind-set to receive new ideas. But look at Anne, a delightful ninety-year-old. The first time we met her she said, "I know I'm not saved, but I still want to be. Even at my age, I want to be. I know I'm not saved because I'm not joyful; I'm just silly." She had a precious sense of humor, able to laugh at her own forgetfulness or physical disabilities and also able to tease playfully with her friends. She realized that this was a surface happiness and that she still lacked the deeper and more meaningful joy found in salvation.

The gospel has a universal appeal to all ages—teens through the elderly—all races, and both sexes. It has the answer to those who are so deep in sinful activities that they've lost all hope of becoming productive, useful, or worthy people. They can be renewed, re-created in Jesus. It also has the answer for those who are living morally pure, kind, generous, loving life-styles. They lack only the finishing touch—the cleansing of Jesus' blood. Never be guilty of overlooking anyone as a likely candidate for salvation.

The Power Is of God

In recounting his conversion, Paul stressed the importance of God: "But when God. . . ." He knew that God's power made a difference in his life, and this belief affected his ministry for years to come. When Paul went to Corinth, he was very frightened, but the Lord assured him of His protection. "One night the Lord spoke to Paul in a vision: 'Do not be afraid; keep on speaking, do not be silent. For I am with you, and no one is going to attack and harm you, because I have many people in this city' " (Acts 18:9-10). Even though his ministry had the elements of fear and much trembling (1 Corinthians 2:3), he had confidence that his message was the power of God (1 Corinthians 1:18, 24; 2:4). When Paul referred to the gospel, he knew the power rested in God: "But we have this treasure in jars of clay to show that this all-surpassing power is from God and not from us" (2 Corinthians 4:7).

Christians need to trust in the message of the gospel rather than in the methods of man. People who are strong, talented, intelligent, and very capable can accomplish so much on their own power that they sometimes go through much of life without ever having to depend on God. Sooner or later, however, a major crisis or trauma renders them helpless. Then they turn to God and depend on His power.

Obedient Spirit

When Paul was convinced of the error of his way, his attitude was one of submissive obedience to the direction of God. He asked, "What shall I do, Lord?" (Acts 22:10). This submissive spirit directed him to the city of Damascus where he fasted (Acts 9:9) and prayed (Acts 9:11) for three days.

This obedient spirit is also seen in his response to the teaching of Ananias. Ananias explained why he had come and told Paul what to do.

A man named Ananias came to see me. He was a devout observer of the law and highly respected by all the Jews living there. He stood beside me and said, "Brother Saul, receive your sight!" And at that very moment I was able to see him. Then he said: "The God of our fathers has chosen you to know his will and to see the Righteous One and to hear words from his mouth. You will be his witness to all men of what you have seen and heard. And now what are you waiting for? Get up, be baptized and wash your sins away, calling on his name" (Acts 22:12-16).

Paul "immediately" obeyed what he had been told (Acts 9:18); in essence, Paul was "calling on his name" (Acts 22:16b).

Many in the religious world are wrong when they equate "calling on his name" with praying to the Lord.

47

Paul's conversion clarifies this point of confusion because Paul had been praying for three days and then was told to be baptized "calling on his name"; hence, praying and "calling on his name" are not the same. Calling on His name is connected with doing what He says. "Not everyone who says to me, 'Lord, Lord,' will enter the kingdom of heaven, but only he who does the will of my Father who is in heaven" (Matthew 7:21). "Why do you call me, 'Lord, Lord,' and do not do what I say?" (Luke 6:46).

Purpose of Conversion

Your conversion affects not only your salvation but also the salvation of many others. Paul knew he had been saved in order to be involved in saving others. Because he had been converted, he wanted others to be converted. The result of his preaching to the lost was praise for God: "And they praised God because of me" (1:24). Paul's conversion will always be living proof of the power of God and the validity of the resurrection of Jesus.

God's power is practical. Changes that are humanly impossible are divinely possible.

Thought Questions for Chapter Six

1. Summarize the conversion of Paul as recorded in Acts 9, 22, and 26.
2. What impact did his conversion have on the church?
3. Why was Paul so effective in his preaching and evangelistic work?
4. What keeps you from reaching out to non-Christians?

5. When sharing your faith, would you be most intimidated by someone older than you? Younger? A different race? Handicapped? Professional? Intellectual? Very rich? Very poor?

CHAPTER
SEVEN

APOSTLE OF LIBERTY
—PART II

B. Apostle by Human Approval (2:1-10)

This is the second in the series of three arguments
for the authenticity of Paul's apostleship. The previous
section stressed Paul's independence, but this one
argues that Paul's gospel was identical to that of the
other apostles. Their approval of Paul's view of Titus
becomes a crucial statement of the truth of his gospel.

1. Paul met with Jerusalem leaders (2:1-2). "Fourteen years later I went up again to Jerusalem, this time
with Barnabas. I took Titus along also. I went in
response to a revelation and set before them the gospel
that I preach among the Gentiles. But I did this
privately to those who seemed to be leaders, for fear
that I was running or had run my race in vain."

One of the historical problems of the Galatian letter
is identifying this particular visit to Jerusalem. The
book of Acts records that Paul made five visits to
Jerusalem: (1) attempt to join the disciples (9:26-30); (2)
famine visit (11:27-30); (3) Jerusalem council (15:1-30);
(4) end of second journey (18:22); and (5) final visit
before imprisonment (21:15-23). Since Paul was attempting to be exact in his chronology (note use of
epeita in Galatians 1:18, 21; 2:1), it is feasible to believe

that the visit in Galatians 2:1 is the same as the one in Acts 11:27-30. Two other pieces of evidence tend to confirm this conclusion. First, Barnabas was present on the trip described in Galatians 2:1 and Acts 11:27-30. According to Galatians, Titus came along on the trip, but he isn't mentioned in either Acts 11:27-30 or Acts 15:1-30. Had the trip noted in Galatians 2:1 been the same as the one noted in Acts 15:1-30, Titus would have entered into the discussion logically. Second, the Acts 11:27-30 trip was to help the needy, which was one of the admonitions the Jerusalem leaders had given Paul (Galatians 2:10).

There is always the possibility that Luke didn't record this visit in Acts. However, the second best possibility is that this is the trip Paul and Barnabas took to Jerusalem for the council meeting (Acts 15) since the subject matter is the same. The meeting mentioned in Galatians 2:2 could refer to a private meeting with the apostles before the big meeting of Acts 15. In Galatians 2:2, Paul stated that he had been preaching among the Gentiles, which would fit the Acts 13–14 journey, so the Jerusalem meeting would be the one recorded in Acts 15. Building a chronology of Paul's visits to Jerusalem isn't easy and can't be done without some assumptions and guesses. (A suggested chronology of Paul's life and writings by Rob McRay is in the Appendix.) However, identifying the meeting isn't as important as observing the decision the leaders made about Paul.

The fourteen years mentioned in verse 1 present a calculation problem. Should those years include the three years prior to the Jerusalem visit, or should they be considered fourteen years after the first visit? Evidence is inconclusive.

This is the first mention of Barnabas in the letter. He was one of the great leaders of the early church.

His being with Paul lent credence to Paul's view of the gospel. A Hebrew Christian with a Levitical background (Acts 4:36-37), Barnabas was generous with his wealth. When no one else willingly accepted Paul, Barnabas became his letter of recommendation to the Jerusalem brethren. He was a leader of the church in Antioch and sought Paul's assistance in the work (Acts 11:23-26). He is described as a good man, full of the Holy Spirit and faith (Acts 11:24).

When Paul needed a companion for the first preaching tour, Barnabas became his faithful partner. He asked for a second chance for a young man named John Mark, and when Paul wouldn't agree, Barnabas took Mark to Cyprus. Apparently, Mark's actions shattered Paul's confidence in him, so Paul was reluctant to take him again. However, Barnabas's work with John Mark restored Paul's confidence in the young man, and as a result, the imprisoned Paul asked for Mark: "Only Luke is with me. Get Mark and bring him with you, because he is helpful to me in my ministry" (2 Timothy 4:11).

These references to Barnabas graphically illustrate the impact this quiet, unassuming man had on the early church and her leaders. With his background, it is understandable why Paul was later so disappointed in Barnabas's actions (Galatians 2:13).

In addition to Barnabas, Titus was with Paul. Since Titus isn't mentioned anywhere in Acts, it is difficult to fit him into the chronological framework. Paul took full responsibility for Titus's being in Jerusalem. He was to serve as a test case to determine who was right—Paul or the Judaizers. Titus was a saved, uncircumcised Gentile. If the Jerusalem leaders approved of him, Paul would win his case.

There are three reasons for Paul's trip to Jerusalem. First, the Judaizers in Antioch claimed to have been sent from Jerusalem with the leaders' approval (Acts 15:2, 24). These could have been the people Paul referred to as "false brothers [who] had infiltrated our ranks" (Galatians 2:4). Antioch seemed to be a hotbed for this problem, in light of Peter's conduct there (which is addressed later in this chapter).

Second, Paul went to Jerusalem because he had received a revelation. The source or place of this revelation isn't discussed.

Third, Paul wanted to tell the leaders the message he was preaching. He used three different descriptions to refer to the leaders: "those who seemed to be leaders" (2:2), "those who seemed to be important" (2:6), and "those reputed to be pillars" (2:9). These references were intended to contrast the credibility the Judaizers no doubt received when they told the Galatians, "We are from Jerusalem" (Acts 15:2, 24). Paul also had direct contact with the Jerusalem leaders. His willingness to lay his message before them didn't mean that he lacked confidence in what he was preaching, for the previous material showed that he knew his message was from God. The question he placed before the leaders concerned his effectiveness as a messenger to the Gentiles. Did he need to do anything differently? He was seeking advice and approval, which he received (2:6, 9-10). Upon his arrival in Jerusalem, Paul met privately with the leaders to make his actions known so there would be no misunderstanding about his work.

2. An incident concerning Titus (2:3-5). "Yet not even Titus, who was with me, was compelled to be circumcised, even though he was a Greek. This matter arose because some false brothers had infiltrated our ranks to spy on the freedom we have in Christ Jesus and to make us slaves. We did not give in to them for a moment, so that the truth of the gospel might remain with you." Titus was a test case to determine whether one had to be circumcised to be saved (Acts 15:1).

In Timothy's case, Paul believed he should be circumcised in order to be more effective among the Jews: "Paul wanted to take him along on the journey, so he circumcised him because of the Jews who lived in that area, for they all knew that his father was a Greek" (Acts 16:3). Paul wasn't opposed to circumcision if one could be more effective as a witness (1 Corinthians 9:22), but he didn't see it as being essential for salvation since the gospel is sufficient to save.

The problem of circumcising Gentile Christians arose in Jerusalem. Paul stated that false brethren who had infiltrated their ranks were the source of the problem (2 Corinthians 11:26). The passive verb indicates that they had been brought in or planted from the outside. The Judaizers of Antioch were leading suspects for this infiltration. Their purposes were clear: spying and slavery. These false brothers were seeking evidence of Paul's disdain or disregard for the law of Moses. The Jews had ritualistic requirements of the law of Moses (4:22-31; 5:1, 13). The false brethren intended to make the Gentile Christians return to a form of slavery (4:9, 19; 5:1).

Paul emphatically stated, "We did not give in to them for a moment, so that the truth of the gospel might remain with you" (2:5). The phrase "truth of the gospel" is also used in his rebuke of Peter (2:14). This phrase means either that the truth is the gospel or that it is truth belonging to the gospel. Truth is an essential part of the gospel. The gospel denies the need for any human effort (such as circumcision) as being essential to salvation, and the gospel does not need to be supplemented. Paul yielded on matters of policy but never principle. He was willing to yield to weak brothers (1 Corinthians 8:13) but not to false brothers.

3. *Paul's relationship with the Jerusalem apostles (2:6-10).* There were three results of Paul's meeting with the Jerusalem leaders. First, the Jerusalem leaders added nothing to his message: "As for those who seemed to be important—whatever they were makes no difference to me; God does not judge by external appearance—those men added nothing to my message" (2:6). Paul's reference to the leaders might be an effort to play down the emphasis that his opponents had made about being from Jerusalem and knowing the "leaders." The leaders agreed that Paul had been given the special task of preaching the gospel to the Gentiles (1 Corinthians 9:2) as Peter was given the task of preaching to the Jews (2:7). Paul affirmed that God was as much at work in his ministry as He was in Peter's ministry (2:8).

A second result was that Paul and Barnabas received the right hand of fellowship: "James, Peter and John, those reputed to be pillars, gave me and Barnabas the right hand of fellowship when they recognized the grace given to me. They agreed that we should go to the Gentiles, and they to the Jews" (2:9). The leaders were in complete agreement that Paul's mission was to the Gentiles.

A third result of the Jerusalem meeting was a request to remember the poor: "All they asked was that we should continue to remember the poor, the very thing I was eager to do" (2:10). Paul eagerly accepted this admonition. It should be noted that Paul switched from "we" to "I." This change supports the idea that this was the Acts 15 meeting and that Barnabas and Paul parted company after the meeting.

This second argument in establishing Paul's apostleship showed total agreement of the leaders of

Jerusalem with his actions and message. Paul had a friendly relationship with the leaders, and they were mutually supportive of one another.

C. Apostle by Action (2:11-21)

This is the third argument for Paul's apostleship and deals with his reaction to Peter—an undeniable church leader and a genuine apostle.

1. Paul confronted Peter (2:11). "When Peter came to Antioch, I opposed him to his face, because he was clearly in the wrong." In the NASV, this verse begins with "but when," showing the inconsistency of Peter's actions in light of the leaders' decision. Christianity came to Antioch, the site of this conflict, after the death of Stephen. Antioch later became the center for missionary activity among the Gentiles (Acts 13:1-3). If the meeting of 2:1-10 is the same as the one in Acts 15:1-30, the incident with Peter took place prior to the second journey and after the Acts 15 meeting.

Paul's opposing Peter to his face is evidence of Paul's status as a genuine apostle. The word *oppose* has a military and political meaning—"resisting an attack." Paul saw Peter's conduct as an attack on the gospel. When he said that Peter "was clearly in the wrong," he meant that Peter "stood condemned" (NASV). The verdict of Peter's action was determined by the act itself.

2. Peter's conduct (2:12-13). "Before certain men came from James, he used to eat with the Gentiles. But when they arrived, he began to draw back and separate himself from the Gentiles because he was afraid of those who belonged to the circumcision group. The other Jews joined him in his hypocrisy, so that by their hypocrisy even Barnabas was led astray."

When Peter was in Antioch, he had the habit of eating with the Gentiles. Eating with others in the first century indicated fellowship and an acceptance of one another. Peter had many opportunities to eat with Gentile disciples (Acts 11:20), for meals could be shared in homes, at church love feasts, and during the Lord's Supper (1 Corinthians 11:20).

Peter had been thoroughly and directly taught concerning God's acceptance of Gentiles. God used a vision to show him that Gentiles shouldn't be considered unclean (Acts 10:14). As a result of the convincing work in the household of Cornelius, Peter ate with them (Acts 10:23, 48; 11:2). Because Peter couldn't claim ignorance in this area, Paul had reason to be upset with Peter's actions.

"Certain men came from James" (2:12) means they either came directly from James or came from the church of which James was a part. Their reason for coming isn't known, but they could have been seeking money for the poor (2:10). These brethren, because of their fear of eating unclean foods, were shocked to see Jews and Gentiles eating together. Peter gradually began to draw back from eating with the Gentiles. "Draw back" is a military term used to describe a retreat from fear of harm.

What were the reasons for Peter's actions? One reason could have been fear, for the politics of legalism is built on fear. He didn't want to lose the goodwill of certain brethren. He also could have feared Jewish revolutionaries who could harm Jews if they felt they were compromising their religion. Peter's actions could be traced to insincerity. He could have pretended to be motivated by loyalty to the law of Moses, when, in fact, he was just plain afraid of his fellow Jewish Christians. Paul used the word *hypocrisy*, which literally means "to answer from under." This word has its meaning from Greek actors who had more than one role in plays. The actor wore a mask that depicted the person he was portraying, and he "spoke from under it." Fear was a recurring problem for Peter (Matthew 14:27-31; Luke 22:54-62); however, he did experience maturity (1 Peter 2:20; 4:16, 19; 5:10).

The effect of Peter's behavior on others was devastating. Not only were other Jews led away, but "even Barnabas was led astray." Paul's disappointment in Barnabas was obvious. He couldn't believe that a solid Christian like Barnabas could make such a mistake. A tragic situation occurred as a result of the actions of Peter, Barnabas, and other Jews. Christians were hypocritical, violated their consciences for the sake of fear, created disunity, and were guilty of racial discrimination.

3. Paul rebuked Peter (2:14-21). Paul's public rebuke is permeated with strong words. It must be remembered that this is the heart of one of his major arguments for his apostleship. The rebuke was a validation of Paul's apostleship and gave insights into the nature and implications of the gospel.

The rebuke consisted of four separate arguments. The first argument is one of consistency. "When I saw that they were not acting in line with the truth of the gospel, I said to Peter in front of them all, 'You are a Jew, yet you live like a Gentile and not like a Jew. How is it, then, that you force Gentiles to follow Jewish customs?' " (2:14). In 2:7, the Jerusalem leaders were depicted as ones who "saw," and Paul used the same wording with respect to himself—he "saw" what Peter was doing. Paul described Peter as one who was "not walking a straight line"; he didn't stay parallel to the truth of the gospel. Peter was a Jew by birth but had lived like a non-Jew. His actions violated the Jewish demands for ceremonial cleansing, pressured Gentiles by withholding fellowship, and raised doubts of God's acceptance of all men. "Jewish customs" refers to the clean and unclean laws of the Jews, written and oral. Peter's conduct demonstrates the danger of brotherhood politics, the struggle to gain control over the interpretation, policies, and beliefs of others. Brotherhood politics destroy personal convictions (Acts 15:9), fellowship, and truth (2:5, 14).

The second argument of the rebuke pertains to justification by faith. "We who are Jews by birth and not 'Gentile sinners' know that a man is not justified by observing the law, but by faith in Jesus Christ. So we, too, have put our faith in Christ Jesus that we may be justified by faith in Christ and not by observing the law, because by observing the law no one will be justified" (2:15-16). The Jews viewed Gentiles as "sinners" since they were born outside the covenant, were lawless (Romans 2:12), and were without God (Ephesians 2:12). The principle is declared: you are "not justified by observing the law, but by faith in Jesus Christ." To be justified means to be declared righteous. In court terms, charges would be dropped because of lack of evidence. "Observing the law" means performing with the expectation of meriting a right standing.

Not only is the justification principle true, but Peter's and Paul's experience declared it to be correct—"so we, too." Since Peter knew the truth, there was no excuse for his actions. He violated the basic principle of the gospel.

The third argument of the rebuke pertains to a misunderstanding of the place of the law (2:17-19). The Judaizers believed that abandoning the law was a sin, but Paul was teaching justification by Christ apart from the law. Since Paul was functioning under Christ's direction, this would make Christ (in the Judaizers' view) an agent of sin. "If, while we seek to be justified in Christ, it becomes evident that we ourselves are sinners, does that mean that Christ promotes sin? Absolutely not!" (2:17). Because Peter had separated himself from Gentiles, he declared by his action that unity between Gentile and Jew was sinful. This wasn't the unity Jesus taught.

The fourth argument of the rebuke pertains to the gospel and God's grace (2:19-21). Since it is difficult to determine where the rebuke actually ends, this section may not be directly related to the rebuke. However, it does have a bearing on the "truth of the gospel" that Peter had violated. This section further explains the law and the life produced by the gospel of grace.

Paul explained what the law did: "For through the law I died to the law so that I might live for God" (2:19). The law killed Paul and brought him despair. This failure directed him to God as a source of deliverance (Romans 7:25). Paul left a works-righteousness religion for the one offered by Jesus. "I have been crucified with Christ and I no longer live, but Christ lives in me. The life I live in the body, I live by faith in the Son of God, who loved me and gave himself for me" (2:20). The law no longer had a claim on Paul because of his cocrucifixion with Jesus. The indwelling Christ became the dynamic for his existence. The new life is lived by faith in the Son of God who showed His love by His sacrifice.

The law had only the ability to kill; it couldn't resurrect a dead man. A dead man can't respond to the advantages of breathing and to a lecture on the benefits of exercise—he is dead! It's the gospel of Jesus Christ that promises resurrection power. Paul spoke of this power in Ephesians 1:18-20:

I pray also that the eyes of your heart may be enlightened in order that you may know the hope to which he has called you, the riches of his glorious inheritance in the saints, and his incomparably great power for us who believe. That power is like the working of his mighty strength, which he exerted in Christ when he raised him from the dead and seated him at his right hand in the heavenly realms.

In his prayer for the Ephesians, Paul referred to power and how it set the stage for the powerful resurrection of the Christian and his being placed in a new position. "But because of his great love for us, God, who is rich in mercy, made us alive with Christ even when we were dead in transgressions—it is by grace you have been saved. And God raised us up with Christ and seated us with him in the heavenly realms in Christ Jesus" (Ephesians 2:4-6).

The law only condemns; it never rewards good. When the state trooper pulls you over, what is your first thought? *What did I do?* What would be your reaction if he congratulated you and gave you a prize for complying with the speed limit? *Unbelievable!* Usually, he pulls you over to condemn, not to commend. If he does catch you violating the law, no amount of "obediences" to other laws will atone for this one violation. Herein lies the deficiency of a justification-by-works system—it will always condemn because of man's weakness.

A photographer returned pictures to a preacher who responded, "These pictures don't do me justice." The photographer remarked, "Sir, you don't need justice; you need mercy!" Paul explains mercy in Titus 3:3-7:

At one time we too were foolish, disobedient, deceived and enslaved by all kinds of passions and pleasures. We lived in malice and envy, being hated and hating one another. But when the kindness and love of God our Savior appeared, he saved us, not because of righteous things we had done, but because of his mercy. He saved us through the washing of rebirth and renewal by the Holy Spirit, whom he poured out on us generously through Jesus Christ our Savior, so that, having been justified by his grace, we might become heirs having the hope of eternal life.

You must choose to live either by law or by faith. "I do not set aside the grace of God, for if righteousness could be gained through the law, Christ died for nothing!" (2:21). Grace nullified the law, and faith nullified meritorious works (Romans 3:27-31). Peter's actions (withdrawing from eating with the Gentiles) showed the need for the gospel and the insufficiency of the law.

The redemption and justification of the Christian rests in the completed work of Christ. It doesn't rest in your right attitude toward the Bible (which you should have), nor does it rest in your determination to be a restorationist (which you should be). There are many good attitudes and actions that would rightfully stem from your justification, but they aren't the grounds or the means of that justification. The focus on the work of God is clearly seen in the book of Galatians. If we focus on something other than Jesus (the work of God), our Christianity will be unbalanced. The emphasis should not be on God's actions (grace) or on man's response (faith), but should be on the focal point of all history—Jesus. Christ in the Christian is the core of the gospel. "To them God has chosen to make known among the Gentiles the glorious riches of this mystery, which is Christ in you, the hope of glory" (Colossians 1:27).

Justification is three-dimensional. Essentially, it begins with a restored, trusting relationship with God. It proceeds to a day-to-day implementation among those with whom you live. Your "talk" of justification should influence your "walk." Finally, you must see justification as an ongoing process (1 John 1:7) because you continually stand justified in God's sight. Your "religion" must be more than a list of facts; it must be seen in your life (5:22-23).

The close of chapter 2 ends the first major section of the letter to the Galatians—the defense of Paul's apostleship. With his credibility intact, Paul entered into the polemic section (chapters 3 and 4) of what the gospel is all about—being saved by faith versus being saved by law.

Application for Today

Paul's meeting with the leaders of the Jerusalem church (2:2, 6) provides several insights into his ministry. The first one has to do with his willingness to let his ministry be examined by others and his openness to change anything that was wrong. Church leaders need to open the message they preach for inspection by others. It is not the intention of any Christian to preach a false gospel, so a periodic inspection is necessary.

A second insight into Paul's ministry would be to observe his opponents. His greatest opponents were not from the pagan world but were false brethren who functioned within (2:4). Christians today need to be aware that false teachers can be in the church and can even claim to be teaching with the approval of other church leaders. "We have heard that some went out from us without our authorization and disturbed you, troubling your minds by what they said" (Acts 15:24).

A third insight is that Paul was willing to act on suggestions he had been given. The Jerusalem leaders added nothing to his message (2:6) and gave him the right hand of fellowship (2:9). They did urge him to remember the poor, and he received this suggestion with eagerness (2:10). Christians need to be willing to accept suggestions from others and to see areas where they have been lacking. Because it is not always easy for the individual Christian to see himself as objectively as he needs to, the help of other loving, concerned Christians is helpful.

Paul's second major argument for his credibility concerns his actions in reference to Peter. Paul was upset over what he considered to be an act of hypocrisy. The strongest condemnation ever given by Jesus was not to the prostitutes, drunkards, or homosexuals but to the religious leaders who appeared one way but were nothing more than hypocrites (Matthew 23). A religion of pretense is repulsive to God. Your reputation should be backed up by your life (Revelation 3:1).

There is a difference between weakness and hypocrisy. The weak are willing to admit their frailties and seek help. Hypocrisy is a cover-up. How many young people have left the Lord because of hypocrisy seen in the church, school, or home? Young people might differ with the judgment of the members of the older generation and still respect them, but they have no use for anyone who is not "real."

The tragedy of hypocrisy is the damage it does to others. In the case of Peter, he influenced other Jews and even Paul's close friend, Barnabas. The power of one man's example is clear. How many people will see the Lord and how many people will be turned away from Him because of good or bad examples?

Peter's wrong actions resulted from attempting to seek the approval of men rather than the approval of God. Brotherhood politics are wrong when truth is sacrificed. The Christian must decide "what" is right and not "who" is right. Consequences cannot be weighed when deciding a course of action—what is right in the sight of God must be the determining factor.

What lessons do you glean from the Lord's example of going among the publicans and sinners at the risk of His reputation (Luke 15:1-2)? Some might say that we need to guard our influence, image, or reputation, but why guard something you never plan to use in a righteous cause? We must live by the standard, "It is never wrong to do right."

These two arguments for Paul's ministry give food for thought for us today, especially for those who are full-time ministers.

Thought Questions for Chapter Seven

1. Would unity in the body of Christ be better promoted by meetings with other brethren?
2. What should the ministry of the church be today?
3. How should we consider the admonition to "remember the poor"?
4. What were the results of Peter's hypocrisy? Of ours?
5. Should pressure be exerted on others to make them do something that they do not feel perfectly good about?

CHAPTER
EIGHT

DOCTRINE OF LIBERTY (SAVED BY GRACE, NOT LAW) —PART I

In this section, Paul was at his "polemic best." He gave six arguments for salvation by grace.

A. Argument from Personal Experience (3:1-5)

Paul began by using the Galatians' conversion experience. One of the ancient rabbinical methods of teaching was to ask a series of questions. (Jesus used this method when He was in the temple [Luke 2:46].) Paul fired a series of questions designed to establish the superiority of grace over law.

1. "Who has bewitched you?" (3:1). "You foolish Galatians! Who has bewitched you? Before your very eyes Jesus Christ was clearly portrayed as crucified." Paul's opening statement—"You foolish Galatians!"— got their attention. (The NEB reads, "You stupid Galatians!") "Foolish" meant spiritually dull (Luke 24:25). Paul used their name (Galatians) for emphasis (see 2 Corinthians 6:11; Philippians 4:15). "Bewitched you" is a phrase used only this one time in the New Testament and should be translated, "who gave you the evil eye?"

Paul preached Jesus Christ as crucified (1 Corinthians 2:1-5). "Before your very eyes" picks up on the metaphor of the "evil eye." The Galatians had taken their eyes off Jesus and had caught the false teachers' eyes. "Clearly portrayed" means to write publicly as on a placard or billboard. Paul considered preaching Christ crucified as the power of God (1 Corinthians 1:18, 24; 2:2, 5). "The gospel is not good advice to men, but good news about Christ; not an invitation to us to do anything, but a declaration of what God has done; not a demand, but an offer."[1] "As crucified" translates as a perfect passive participle expressing a historical fact with continuing results. Jesus' work is still being felt by men today and continues to be a substitute for sin. Nothing picks up where the cross stops because it never stops. The cross is continual proof of man's inability to save himself. "Through him everyone who believes is justified from everything you could not be justified from by the law of Moses" (Acts 13:39).

True gospel preaching must center in God's redemptive work at the cross. Is it possible that pulpits are filled with more preaching on Paul than on Jesus? Where are the pages of Bibles the most worn? Do adult Bible study classes include all the "modern" subjects but neglect a Christ-centered curriculum? How can the present-day disciple have Christ formed in him (4:19) with so little knowledge of the One who is his Lord?

2. "Did you receive the Spirit by observing the law, or by believing what you heard?" (3:2). The opening line—"I would like to learn just one thing from you"—shows Paul's intense emotions. You can feel that his statement is made "tongue in cheek." After

---

[1]John R. W. Stott, *The Message of Galatians* (London: Inter-Varsity Press, 1968), p. 70.

stating he would like to learn one thing, he asks *four* questions!

He questions the way the Galatians had become Christians. Did they receive the Spirit as a result of law or as a result of "hearing with faith" (NASV)? The Spirit is given to all who become Christians (Acts 2:38; 5:32; Ephesians 1:13-14). Man's role in the redemptive process is to receive, not to seize or achieve (Acts 2:41; 1 Corinthians 4:7; 15:3).

3. *"Are you so foolish? After beginning with the Spirit, are you now trying to attain your goal by human effort?" (3:3).* "Are you so foolish?" reflects the same idea as the opening phrase in 3:1—"You foolish Galatians." The antithesis of this verse is "Spirit" and "human effort" ("flesh," NASV). Paul said that you can't begin one way and end in another. The Judaizers taught that something had to be added to faith to complete the maturing process. Since human effort didn't begin the process, neither can it complete it. Salvation is the work of God from beginning to end.

4. *"Have you suffered so much for nothing?" (3:4).* Paul urged his readers not to waste all the experiences they had had in Christ. "Suffered" can be translated two different ways. One interpretation uses the word in the sense of affliction; therefore, they endured much in becoming Christians (KJV; NASV; NIV). A second interpretation views "suffer" in the sense of experiences, i.e., the blessings they have received (RSV; NEB). The former translation fits the flow of questions and the entire tenor of the book.

5. *"Does God give you his Spirit and work miracles among you because you observe the law, or because you believe what you heard?" (3:5).* This question attempts to summarize verses 1-5 and strongly reflects the question posed in 3:2. Miracles were used to show God's approval. "The whole assembly became silent as they listened to Barnabas and Paul telling about the miraculous signs and wonders God had done among the Gentiles through them" (Acts 15:12).

Man's role is to receive while God's role is to give. When we ask God to meet our needs, He is honored (Matthew 6:25-34; 7:7-11; James 1:5-8). Christians should respond to God's blessings with thanksgiving (2 Corinthians 9:6-15; 1 Timothy 4:1-5). God is dishonored when we think that we need to help Him and that He owes us an expression of gratitude for our help (Psalm 50:7-13; Acts 17:24-25).

B. Argument from Old Testament (3:6-14)

We don't know the arguments that Paul's opponents used to get the Galatians to accept a "different gospel," but they probably used the Old Testament, especially Abraham. Paul used the Old Testament and Abraham to support the gospel he preached; his emphasis provided strong validation for his gospel. He alluded to the Old Testament in the following verses: 3:6 (Genesis 15:6); 3:8 (Genesis 12:3; 18:18; 22:18); 3:10 (Deuteronomy 27:26); 3:11 (Habakkuk 2:4); 3:12 (Leviticus 18:5); 3:13 (Deuteronomy 21:23).

1. Abraham was justified by faith (3:6-9). "Consider Abraham: 'He believed God, and it was credited to him as righteousness' " (Galatians 3:6). This is a key verse in Paul's argument for salvation by grace. The heart of this argument is that Abraham was considered righteous (Genesis 15:6) *before* the covenant of circumcision was given in Genesis (chapter 17) and some 430 years before the law of Moses was given (Galatians 3:17). Hence, neither the covenant of circumcision nor the law of Moses was essential for his salvation.

A closer look at Genesis 15:6 reveals that Abraham wasn't on the mountaintop in his faith; on the contrary, his faith was at a low ebb. Abraham was concerned about being childless (Genesis 15:1-3). God responded by repeating the promise that Abraham's offspring would be as countless as the stars (Genesis 15:5). It's at this point in Abraham's belief that God credited him as righteous. Abraham's being credited as righteous was the result of a benevolent and gracious God rather than Abraham's being an awesome man of faith!

God reaffirmed His promise in Genesis 17:2: "I will confirm my covenant between me and you and will greatly increase your numbers." During this reaffirmation, God also changed Abram's name to Abraham. *Abram* means "father," and *am* is the Hebrew word for "peoples or nations"; hence, he is the father of nations. It should be noted that God said, "For I have made you a father of many nations" (17:5), when Abraham didn't even have one child! Paul used this verse in Romans 4:17 to show God's power to declare a thing to be, even though it may not presently exist.

In addition to changing Abraham's name, God gave him the covenant of circumcision (17:9-14). This covenant can literally be translated, "I will *cut* a covenant." Circumcision was the symbol of the covenant God was "cutting" with Abraham. This covenant distinguished Abraham from the pagan tribes and was a mark of intimacy to remind him of God's presence. However, in time, its symbolism became more important than its reality in the Jewish mind, especially to the Pharisees who were "separatists" in heart. The Judaizers argued that this covenant was everlasting and needed to be followed by all spiritual descendants to this day. It's true that the covenant was described as "everlasting" (17:13), but God had the right to change it.

Besides Abraham's name change and the covenant of circumcision, his wife's name, Sarai, was changed to Sarah. "As for Sarai your wife, you are no longer to call her Sarai; her name will be Sarah. I will bless her and will surely give you a son by her. I will bless her so that she will be the mother of nations; kings of peoples will come from her" (17:15-16).

Abraham's story reveals that even a great man of faith sometimes doubts and doesn't trust God completely. After the promise that he would become the father of nations, Abraham and Sarah became impatient and took matters into their own hands. "Now Sarai, Abram's wife, had borne him no children. But she had an Egyptian maidservant named Hagar; so she said to Abram, 'The LORD has kept me from having children. Go, sleep with my maidservant; perhaps I can build a family through her.' Abram agreed to what Sarai said" (Genesis 16:1-2). Ishmael was born, but God rejected this alternate plan since Ishmael was a child by their fleshly power and not a child by the promise of God. Using the background of the Galatians as a basis, Paul showed how Abraham tried to attain his goal (having children) by human effort, which wasn't acceptable to God (offspring were to be His gift). Abraham had to trust in the God of the impossible who gives life to the dead (both Abraham and Sarah were considered dead [Romans 4:19]) and calls things that aren't as though they were (Romans 4:17b). Using Abraham as an example, Paul showed that trust in God, not human effort, produced blessings.

Paul took the Genesis 15:6 promise and explained how people today can become the spiritual children of Abraham: "Understand, then, that those who believe are children of Abraham" (Galatians 3:7). It should now be clear to Paul's readers that they could be Abraham's spiritual children without circumcision, law-keeping, or even a powerful, unwavering faith since Abraham was blessed without all three! However, this isn't easy to say that Abraham had no faith because he did have faith to leave a country under the direction of God (Genesis 12:1). But the blessing rested more on who God was than who Abraham was. In this case, God was the giver, and man, the receiver. Abraham didn't receive based on what he was able to do. His response didn't "earn" him the blessing of God, and his response wasn't equal to God's response. It wasn't a fifty-fifty deal! Abraham's story reinforced Paul's view of man's salvation—it isn't a result of human effort or merit but is a result of the grace of God! Quoting Genesis 15:6 is significant because of the word *believe*. This is the first time the word occurs in Genesis; hence, it is true that Abraham is the father of the faithful (Romans 4:16).

In 3:8, Paul enlarged his thoughts begun in 3:6-7: "The Scripture foresaw that God would justify the Gentiles by faith, and announced the gospel in advance to Abraham: 'All nations will be blessed through you.'" The gospel or good news was "preached" (NASV) or announced in advance to Abraham. The good news was that the blessing given through Abraham included justification of the Gentiles and amounted to the same thing as forgiveness (Acts 3:26). When Paul declared the justification of Gentiles as a part of God's promise to Abraham, he affirmed the salvation of non-law-keeping nations. If God promised in advance the salvation of non-law-keeping people, why do justified Gentiles have to keep the laws and rituals of Moses to be saved? The good news (gospel) for Gentiles is that justification is based on a relationship with God through faith in Christ.

Verse 9 summarizes verse 6-8: "So those who have faith are blessed along with Abraham, the man of faith." "Along with" means that the same blessing (relationship with God) that Abraham had is available to the present-day man of faith. The Galatians were recipients of the same blessing Abraham had—without either circumcision or law-keeping. However, they did need faith in God, which resulted in His declaring them righteous.

Abraham is an example of how all men are saved—through confidence in God, resulting in obedience. Trust and obedience should never be separated. It isn't trust plus obedience, but it's a trust that includes obedience. An illustration from the book of Hebrews shows this correlation. In Hebrews 3:18, the writer declared that disobedience was the reason for the Israelites' failure to enter the promised land, and in the next verse, unbelief is affirmed as the cause of failure: "And to whom did God swear that they would never enter his rest if not to those who disobeyed? So we see that they were not able to enter, because of their unbelief." If disobedience and unbelief are the same, obedience and belief are the same. In other Scriptures, obedience and faith are connected: "Through him and for his name's sake, we received grace and apostleship to call people from among all the Gentiles to the *obedience that comes from faith*" (Romans 1:5, emphasis added); "But now revealed and made known through the prophetic writings by the command of the eternal God, so that all nations might *believe and obey him*" (Romans 16:26, emphasis added).

Abraham's life marvelously illustrates the faith principle. It's obvious that his faith had peaks and valleys. He believed God regarding the promise of Isaac in spite of the odds. "Yet he did not waver through unbelief regarding the promise of God, but was strengthened in his faith and gave glory to God" (Romans 4:20). The hopelessness of the situation ("against all hope" [Romans 4:18]) called for an even greater faith in God. Offering Isaac was an incredible expression of faith in the power of God.

By faith Abraham, when God tested him, offered Isaac as a sacrifice. He who had received the promises was about to sacrifice his one and only son, even though God had said to him, "It is through Isaac that your offspring will be reckoned." Abraham reasoned that God could raise the dead, and figuratively speaking, he did receive Isaac back from death (Hebrews 11:17-19).

Abraham's faith in God motivated him to build altars and worship God (Genesis 12:7-8).

However, Abraham didn't always live on the high mountains of faith. The story of Sodom and Gomorrah shows that Abraham was upset and confused about God.

Then Abraham approached him [the Lord] and said: "Will you sweep away the righteous with the wicked? What if there are fifty righteous people in the city? Will you really sweep it away and not spare the place for the sake of the fifty righteous people in it? Far be it from you to do such a thing—to kill the righteous with the wicked, treating the righteous and the wicked alike. Far be it from you! Will not the Judge of all the earth do right?" (Genesis 18:23-25).

Abraham questioned the nature and heart of God. When he saw that God was agreeable to saving the city for ten righteous people, Abraham knew God was kind and merciful (Genesis 18:32).

Another illustration of Abraham's lack of belief concerns his wife, Sarah. Abraham lied on two different occasions—to Pharaoh (Genesis 12:18) and to Abimelech (Genesis 20:2)—that Sarah was his sister. Can you imagine the man of faith, the father of the faithful, lying? How could God save a liar and one who doubted His nature and questioned His actions? God saved Abraham because of the overall direction of his life! These isolated cases of sin weren't characteristic of his life. If God judges men by isolated acts, no one will be saved. Abraham is an example of a less-than-perfect law-keeper who was saved; therefore, Christians don't have to have perfect faith any more than Abraham had perfect faith. The bottom line of salvation has always been the same since the beginning of time—man is saved by grace in spite of, not because of, his deeds. Whether Abraham had "forensic righteousness" (because God said so) or he had "bestowed righteousness" (because God gave it), he was nonetheless righteous in God's eyes (Romans 4:1-8).

2. Curse of the law (3:10-14). The second half of Paul's argument from the Old Testament pertains to the curse of the law. The background for this argument is quoted in Deuteronomy 27 where the Levites recited to the people of Israel the cursings given to those who disobey. The final cursing about the man who didn't uphold the words of the law by carrying them out (Deuteronomy 27:26) is alluded to in 3:10. The people of Israel had changed the law from a national guide to a self-redemptive system.

Paul used Deuteronomy 27:26 to conclude that no one is justified by the law because of his inability to keep it: "Clearly no one is justified before God by the law, because, 'The righteous will live by faith' " (3:11). His answer was also scriptural since it was a quotation from Habakkuk 2:4. Faith, rather than law-keeping, must be the way of salvation because of man's disobedient nature. The law doesn't accept faith as a grounds of justification; it accepts only actions. Paul emphasized this when he quoted Leviticus 18:5 to the Galatians: "The law is not based on faith; on the

75

contrary, 'The man who does these things will live by them' '' (3:12). If doing or performing is the basis for receiving eternal life, the law-keeper will never receive it because he can't be a perfect law-keeper. The law makes no provision for disobedience. It's a self-condemning system because it's man-centered rather than God-centered.

Enter the work of Christ! "Christ redeemed us from the curse of the law by becoming a curse for us, for it is written: 'Cursed is everyone who is hung on a tree.' He redeemed us in order that the blessing given to Abraham might come to the Gentiles through Christ Jesus, so that by faith we might receive the promise of the Spirit" (3:13-14). Jesus redeemed us! Jesus stood under the curse for us. As stated in Deuteronomy 21:22-23, a person hanging on a tree brought a curse to the whole land. Jesus did this for two purposes: (1) so the Gentiles would receive the blessing of Abraham, and (2) so the Jew and the Gentile would receive the promise of the Spirit (3:2; 4:6).

This section (3:10-14) contains a blessing for some and a cursing for others. The ones who are cursed are those who rely on observing the law (3:10) and those who don't do everything written in the law (Deuteronomy 27:26). If the Galatians believed a different gospel that relied on law-keeping as being an essential part of salvation, they were cursed in the process. However, they didn't have to take that route because Jesus had become a curse for them (3:13) and had taken their place. They were now counted among the blessed, based on the principle of faith (3:11b). They were blessed because Christ redeemed them from the curse of the law (3:14). The question for them—and you—is: Why return to a system of condemnation and despair when the work of Christ has made it possible for you to enjoy the blessing of Abraham and the promise of the Spirit without it?

Paul had more to say about the promise of the Spirit (Acts 2:38; 5:32) in the next chapters. The Judaizers used the law as the "force" or power to live the Christian life whereas Paul's emphasis was on the Spirit (5:16, 18, 25). The power for you is Christ living in you (4:19) and your yielding yourself to Him. The power for living the Christian life is Jesus! All of this power is supplied by God.

Paul's closing argument from the Old Testament was especially forceful because it included all the ingredients of the Judaizers' arguments, based on a correct interpretation of the facts. Paul gave them two choices: the way of faith, or the way of the law. The way of faith promised life to the believer, and the way of the law promised life to the doer. The way of faith believes that God can justify, and the way of the law places justification on man's performance. The real difference between the two choices is either trust in the finished work of Christ or trust in self. Paul hoped the Galatians would see the difference and return to the true gospel of grace.

C. Argument from the Purpose of the Law (3:15-29)

Apparently Paul's opponents had argued that the law was superior since it came after the promise to Abraham. Exactly how the Judaizers used the story of Abraham and the law of Moses to prove their case isn't fully known, but Paul used all the available material to support his case and refute their arguments.

1. The law didn't do away with the promise (3:15-18). Paul began this section more calmly by calling the Galatians "brothers" instead of "you foolish Galatians" (3:1) and by using an example from everyday life. "Brothers, let me take an example from everyday life. Just as no one can set aside or add to a human covenant that has been duly established, so it is in this case" (3:15). Since, in everyday life, a human covenant can't be added to or set aside, neither can God's covenant with Abraham. Paul used "promises" because Abraham's promise is mentioned so many times in Scripture (Genesis 12:7; 13:15; 24:7). Paul declared that Abraham wasn't the only beneficiary. The promises were spoken to Abraham *and* to his seed. "The Scripture does not say, 'and to seeds,' meaning many people, but 'and to your seed,' meaning one person, who is Christ" (3:16). God's covenant with Abraham wasn't a mutual covenant because Abraham was asleep when it was made (Genesis 15:12). The covenant with Abraham was based on a unilateral promise from God. Since Abraham didn't have anything to do with its making, he couldn't break it. God was in control! Paul explained "the Seed" to be Jesus (3:19).

Now Paul was ready to drive home the point of this section. "What is meant is this: The law, introduced 430 years later, does not set aside the covenant previously established by God and thus do away with the promise. For if the inheritance depends on the law, then it no longer depends on a promise; but God in his grace gave it to Abraham through a promise" (3:17-18). "What I mean is this" referred to the material in 3:15. Law and promise can't be combined because of their differences. Giving the law of Moses 430 years after Abraham didn't destroy the previous covenant. The purpose for the introduction of the law (3:17a) is further discussed in this chapter, but its purpose was not to discard the covenant made to Abraham. The root word for "gave" in 3:18b is the word for grace; hence, the NIV states, "But God in his grace gave." Using the perfect tense (gave) stressed the permanency of God's action. Man has always been saved by God's grace. Giving the law 430 years later didn't bring about a new means to be saved; it simply hastened the need for man to see his need for the grace of God.

2. The law was temporary and inferior (3:19-20). Paul asked a natural question: What was the purpose of the law? Answer: "It was added because of transgressions until the Seed to whom the promise referred had come" (3:19a). The law was added to the covenant of Abraham to reveal transgressions; i.e., to make them known (Romans 7:7). The limited duration of the law was "until the Seed to whom the promise referred had come." Jesus Christ is clearly the meaning of "Seed" (3:16). The law was given to a limited people (Exodus 19:3-6; 20:1-2; Psalm 147:19-20), for a limited time (until Christ came), and for a limited purpose ("to lead us to Christ" [3:24]).

The law was given not to save but to show the need to be saved by grace rather than performance. The law was a mirror to reflect man's dirtiness, but the law couldn't cleanse man (James 1:22-25). The law was destined to break the backs of all those who tried to obey it and caused them to scream for help (Romans 7:21-25). Law has the ability to bruise, imprison, condemn, kill, humble, and drive to despair all who seek to keep it (Romans 3:20; 4:15; 7:7). A study of salvation by law makes all Christians glad that there is a salvation by grace.

Paul further contrasted the law of Moses with the covenant that God made with Abraham. "The law was put into effect through angels by a mediator. A mediator, however, does not represent just one party; but God is one" (3:19b-20). The law came by angels and Moses, not directly by God as the promise did; therefore, the law was inferior to the promise (Deuteronomy 33:2; Acts 7:53; Hebrews 2:2). The meaning of 3:20 always has been difficult for students of the Word. A mediator implies two parties (God and the people), but the covenant with Abraham didn't demand a mediator.

God's dealings with Abraham and Moses reveal a number of contrasts. Abraham received a promise while Moses received a law. God told Abraham what He would do ("I will") while He told Moses what to do ("thou shalt"). Abraham received a promise he needed to believe while Moses received a law to obey. By contrasting the covenant of Abraham with the law of Moses, Paul hoped his readers would see the difference and make the proper choice. Responsible-thinking Christians won't choose the law when they understand that it is temporary and inferior. The legalistic requirements of the law appealed to man's fleshly nature and were incapable of saving or providing life (3:21).

3. The law put man in prison (3:21-23). Paul didn't want to be guilty of "overkilling" the law of Moses and give the impression that the law opposed the promise. "Is the law, therefore, opposed to the promises of God? Absolutely not! For if a law had been given that could impart life, then righteousness would certainly have come by the law" (3:21). The law showed the need for the promise because no law has ever been given that could impart life. The law is good for the living, but can never make dead men alive. Only a gospel of grace can resurrect the dead by an act of God. Once a man is dead, he has lost his power to live and must depend on something other than himself for life. A series of lectures on the benefit of breathing and walking can be given to a dead man, but he is incapable of responding. Jesus supplies the power to raise the physically and spiritually dead man.

The correlation between the power of Christ's resurrection and the resurrection of one who is dead in transgressions is seen clearly in Ephesians where Paul prayed that his readers would know about this available power.

I pray also that the eyes of your heart may be enlightened in order that you may know the hope to which he has called you, the riches of his glorious inheritance in the saints, and his incomparably great power for us who believe. That power is like the working of his mighty strength, which he exerted in Christ when he raised him from the dead and seated him at his right hand in the heavenly realms (Ephesians 1:18-20).

The parallel to the power in the resurrection of Jesus is shown in Ephesians 2:5-6: "[God] made us alive with Christ even when we were dead in transgressions—it is by grace you have been saved. And God raised us up with Christ and seated us with him in the heavenly realms in Christ Jesus." The power that accomplished the physical resurrection of Jesus is available to spiritually raise you and seat you with Jesus "in the heavenly realms."

The desperate need of man is seen in the fact that he is a prisoner of sin. "But the Scripture declares that the whole world is a prisoner of sin, so that what was promised, being given through faith in Jesus Christ, might be given to those who believe" (3:22). When man determines that he isn't free, he will be drawn to a message of grace promising freedom (5:1). The importance of faith is seen because it is mentioned twice in 3:22—"through faith in Jesus . . . to those who believe."

Man can be enslaved to sin and not know how to get out or even that there is a way out. This prison is fortified by a knowledge of law. "Before this faith came, we were held prisoners by the law, locked up until faith should be revealed" (3:23). Two verbs in the verse show the confining nature of the law. The verb "held prisoners" referred to protecting a city by keeping visitors out and the residents in (2 Corinthians 11:32; Philippians 4:7; 1 Peter 1:5). The second verb, "locked up," means cooped up or hemmed in (Luke 5:6).

The law produced a state of life that man, in his right mind, would never desire. Who wants to be in prison for the rest of his life? If the Galatians bought the gospel of law-keeping, they would return to the prison from which they had escaped. No one has to lecture to imprisoned people about the beauties of freedom. Because they know the despair and boredom of prison life, they have a deeper appreciation for freedom. The law fulfilled its purpose by creating an appreciation for a gospel of freedom.

4. The law prepared for the coming of Christ (3:24-27). Paul likened the law to the *pedagogue*, an entrusted slave who took care of a child from age six to sixteen. This word is translated "in charge to lead" and "supervision." "So the law was put in charge to lead us to Christ that we might be justified by faith. Now that faith has come, we are no longer under the supervision of the law" (3:24-25).

By using *pedagogue*, a term the Galatians understood, Paul was stressing two ideas: (1) the disciplinary nature of law that results in a very regimented life; (2) one is very immature if he still needs this supervisor because he is incapable of handling his freedom. Obedience to law isn't a measure of spiritual maturity—it's just the opposite.

Paul has shown that the law was both our jailer and our tutor (baby-sitter). There was a time when both were needed, but when their purposes were fulfilled, they were no longer required. A person who has practiced justification by law is extremely happy when he discovers justification by faith and God's amazing grace. The one who has tasted the freedom found in justification by faith isn't likely to return to jail or to be placed under a baby-sitter's supervision (*pedagogue* is a combination of two words—child and leader). Paul used all this reasoning to convince the Galatians that they didn't want this new gospel.

The law prepared the world for the coming of Christ who was the fulfillment of Abraham's promise and who would make it possible for all nations to be in the family of God. "You are all sons of God through faith in Christ Jesus" (3:26).

The world can become the sons of God only by faith in Christ Jesus. Paul clearly defined faith when he discussed the life of Abraham. Becoming a son of God isn't a result of "faith in faith," nor in your personal work or performance; it is a result of faith in the work of Christ. The object of your faith is more important than the quality of your faith. A strong faith in a weak bridge will get you wet, but a weak faith in a strong bridge will keep you dry. The object of your faith makes up for the deficiencies of your faith.

Directly connected to faith in Christ Jesus is baptism into Christ. "For all of you who were baptized into Christ have clothed yourselves with Christ" (3:27). When a service begins with "for," it introduces the reason for something. Those who have been brought into union with Christ ("baptized into Christ") have been clothed with Christ. Being clothed with Christ is an interesting image for modern people, but it was a powerful message to the first readers of the letter. In every culture there is a time when a boy becomes a man. For Jewish boys, it is the bar mitzvah (son of the law) on the first Sabbath after reaching age twelve. For the Greeks, a boy became a man at eighteen when his hair was cut off and offered to the gods. In Roman culture, a boy became a man after he burned his toys (see 1 Corinthians 13:11) and received a *toga virilea*. Paul was using similar Roman imagery to show the transfer from the world into the family of God. Just as the transfer into manhood wasn't complete without the toga, entrance into the family of God isn't complete without baptism.

The early church didn't see baptism as separate from faith. It was considered a vital part of faith in Christ. Baptism shouldn't be viewed as a meritorious act that causes God to be in debt; rather, it is a transfer of ownership. God now owns the believer as His child because of the work of Christ on the cross (Romans 6:1-4). Baptism begins a relationship with God through Christ that is an ever-growing process of being clothed with Him more each day. "Rather, clothe yourselves with the Lord Jesus Christ, and do not think about how to gratify the desires of the sinful nature" (Romans 13:14).

Being part of the family of God and one of the heirs of Abraham has great appeal. The choice to be a recipient of the blessing of Abraham is an individual decision. Your relationship with God is brought about not because you are a member of the family of covenant people but because you belong to God. As a result of belonging to God, you automatically belong to the people of the covenant.

5. *The law couldn't create equality, but the promise could (3:28-29).* The first-century world wasn't without its prejudices and discriminatory acts. There were three major class distinctions: race (Jew or Greek), rank

(slave or free), and sex (male or female). Paul declared that such prejudice ended with Jesus. "There is neither Jew nor Greek, slave nor free, male nor female, for you are all one in Christ Jesus" (3:28). Paul didn't say that distinctions no longer exist (for example, there are still males and females), but the promise brought equality. Paul's acknowledgment of equality was proof of his change and conversion.

This entire section (3:6-29) is summarized in 3:29: "If you belong to Christ, then you are Abraham's seed, and heirs according to the promise." The arguments from Abraham and the law are closely related. Paul wanted his readers to understand that obedience to the gospel he preached made them the spiritual children of Abraham and in line for the promise. Implied in this conclusion is the question: What more do you want? There was no need for them to buy another gospel, losing out on the inheritance of Abraham. The Galatians were heirs to the promise and were no longer prisoners awaiting their execution. They were mature with all the privileges of sonship, never needing the restraint of a tutor (*pedagogue*) again. They were sons, not slaves! (Paul pursues the contrast of sonship and slavery in 4:1-7.) The law had its purpose, but it was never intended to be the stopping place and final home for those who sought a relationship with God. This thought is summarized in these words:

Some try to go to Jesus without first meeting Moses. They want to skip the Old Testament to inherit the promise of justification in Christ without the prior pain of condemnation by the law. Others go to Moses and the law to be condemned, but they stay in this unhappy bondage. They are still living in the Old Testament. Their religion is a grievous yoke, hard to be borne. They have never gone to Christ, to be set free.[2]

Circumcision Equals Baptism?

One of the New Testament books that was studied and preached during the Protestant Reformation was Galatians. Since the Protestant Reformation was a reaction against the works-righteousness system of justification developed over the centuries by Roman Catholicism, the message of Galatians was a natural source for theology among the reformers. One of the by-products of their theology was equating the human act of circumcision with the act of baptism. Since sprinkling babies when they were eight days old was the prevailing practice of the Catholics, it was easy to equate it with the act of circumcision. As Paul opposed circumcision to be essential for salvation (Acts 15:1-2) so some today oppose baptism by immersion to be essential for salvation.

The Protestant Reformation also reduced the "seven sacraments" to two (baptism and the Lord's Supper). Hence, baptism became a "work" performed after one became a Christian. When baptism is viewed as a "work" (i.e., what one does), baptism cannot be essential to salvation without violating the basic thesis of Galatians—salvation by grace, not by works.

Paul used circumcision metaphorically to refer to those who were spiritually purified. "No, a man is a Jew if he is one inwardly; and circumcision is circumcision of the heart, by the Spirit, not by the written code. Such a man's praise is not from men, but from God" (Romans 2:29). "For it is we who are the

---
[2]Stott, p. 96.

circumcision, we who worship by the Spirit of God, who glory in Christ Jesus, and who put no confidence in the flesh" (Philippians 3:3).

Even though baptism is performed by men on men, it should not be viewed as a "work," placing God in debt to man. Baptism unites men with Christ. It is a participation in the blessings of His death. "Or don't you know that all of us who were baptized into Christ Jesus were baptized into his death? We were therefore buried with him through baptism into death in order that, just as Christ was raised from the dead through the glory of the Father, we too may live a new life" (Romans 6:3-4). By obeying the command of baptism, you are not "earning" or "working" for anything any more than Joshua "earned" the victory of Jericho when he marched around the walls and they fell down.

It is interesting to observe the composition of Jesus' teaching in Mark 16:15-16. "Go into all the world and preach the good news to all creation. Whoever believes and is baptized will be saved, but whoever does not believe will be condemned." "Whoever believes" is an aorist (past tense in Greek) active participle and "is baptized" is an aorist passive participle. A passive participle indicates something done to a person. If either belief or baptism must be classified as "human works," belief would qualify more than baptism since it is "active" and the latter is "passive."

Circumcision is remotely connected with baptism in Colossians 2:11-13.

In him you were also circumcised, in the putting off of the sinful nature, not with a circumcision done by the hands of men but with the circumcision done by Christ, having been buried with him in baptism and raised with him through your faith in the power of God, who raised him from the dead. When you were dead in your sins and in the uncircumcision of your sinful nature, God made you alive with Christ. He forgave us all our sins.

It is obvious that this is a spiritual circumcision since it was not "done by the hands of men." The purpose of this circumcision was the "putting off of the sinful nature." Prior to this spiritual circumcision, we were dead in our sins, but God made us alive by forgiving our sins. This circumcision was done by Christ through our faith in the power of God and this operation took place when we were "buried with him in baptism."

If you liken baptism to spiritual circumcision, baptism is essential to salvation because without it, there is no "putting off" or "forgiveness of sins." In baptism, your trust is in God and not in what you are doing for yourself. Baptism is an expression of faith and should not be considered an addition to faith.

Application for Today

Chapter 3 begins the major doctrinal section of Galatians. The opening paragraph (3:1-5) is a series of questions that Paul wanted his readers to consider. One question really pinpointed his major concern: "After beginning with the Spirit, are you now trying to attain your goal by human effort?" The following chart contrasts Paul's preaching with that of the false teachers.

True Gospel	*False Gospel*
Justification: Faith	Law
Sanctification: Spirit	Works

The false gospel emphasized human effort from start to finish. When people have the mind-set that you must "earn" what you get, this false gospel has great appeal!

Today we might not be tempted to depend on the same works for redemption, but we can turn Christian activities into works that we believe to be "gaining" God's favor. We should assemble with God's people, read our Bibles, pray, and seek to convert others to the Lord, but should these activities be considered redemptive? Have some of us made the Lord's Supper into an activity that earns the favor of God? Why do some individuals miss Sunday morning Bible classes, come late for the song service, partake of the Lord's Supper, and leave before the preaching?

This chapter stressed the necessity of our being baptized in order to be sons of God and to be clothed with Christ. "You are all sons of God through faith in Christ Jesus, for all of you who were baptized into Christ have clothed yourselves with Christ" (3:26-27). Baptism is not a work of man's own righteousness to earn the approval of God but is a participation and sharing in the death of Christ. "I have been crucified with Christ and I no longer live, but Christ lives in me" (2:20; see Romans 6:3-4). In Mark 16:16 Jesus declared, "Whoever believes and is baptized will be saved, but whoever does not believe will be condemned." "Believes" is an aorist (past tense in Greek) active participle, and "baptized" is an aorist passive participle. Passive denotes being acted upon, not acting. In baptism, the stress isn't as much on what you do as it is on what you are receiving. It doesn't put God into your debt. However, without baptism there can be no sonship or clothing of Christ (3:26-27).

The plan of God to provide redemption for the whole world began to unfold with the life of Abraham. Every Christian should be appreciative of the plan that God has had from the beginning (Ephesians 1:4, 11; 2:15).

The church should never be seen as an afterthought in the mind of God; it is a direct expression of the promise of blessing all nations through Abraham. "His intent was that now, through the church, the manifold wisdom of God should be made known to the rulers and authorities in the heavenly realms" (Ephesians 3:10).

The church should never be viewed as just another organization. The foresight and provisions by God should cause the Christian to feel fortunate that he has been granted, by the grace of God, a chance to share in God's community. Those who are in the church are the sons of God and heirs of the promise. "So you are no longer a slave, but a son; and since you are a son, God has made you also an heir" (4:7).

Thought Questions for Chapter Eight

1. How important is the use of questions in teaching?
2. Can you cite some instances of your faith being tested as Abraham's was?
3. Should we study the Old Testament today? Why or why not?
4. What works do some consider redemptive today?
5. Are you "saved to serve" or "serving to be saved"?

CHAPTER NINE

DOCTRINE OF LIBERTY (SAVED BY GRACE, NOT LAW) —PART II

D. Argument from Superiority of Adoption in Christ (4:1-11)

At the end of chapter 3, Paul illustrated how the law was our "child leader" (supervisor or tutor). In a wealthy Greek home, the child leader was responsible for escorting the child to and from school and other activities. With this illustration Paul slides right into his next major argument for salvation by grace by discussing "guardians and trustees" (4:2).

1. Adoption explained (4:1-7). "What I am saying is that as long as the heir is a child, he is no different from a slave, although he owns the whole estate. He is subject to guardians and trustees until the time set by his father" (4:1-2). Since the child wasn't old enough to control the estate, he was no different from a slave. The son's childhood was a form of bondage (slavery), and since he wasn't old enough to control the estate, it had to be directed and controlled by guardians and trustees. A guardian had the total care of the child, and the trustee looked after financial matters (Romans 16:23; Luke 12:42; 16:1). The estate was the father's promise, and he set the inheritance time. When the boy became a man, he could have the estate (see the discussion of 3:27 as to when this took place).

While the son waited to come of age and receive his inheritance, he was in the slavery of childhood. Paul applied this illustration to man's spiritual condition before Christ. "So also, when we were children, we were in slavery under the basic principles of the world" (4:3). He likened the time before Christ to childhood and slavery to "the basic principles of the world." This phrase has been hard to decipher because of its ambiguity (see Colossians 2:8, 20). It had two different meanings for the Jewish and the Gentile Christians. For the Jewish Christian, it referred to the ABC's of the Jewish system ("elementary truths" [Hebrews 5:12]). Since the law held men in check, they were held in slavery (3:23). For the Gentile Christian, it referred to the belief that the world was controlled by demons and spirits. The pagan Gentile conducted himself properly because of his fear of the spirits. He was enslaved to what he was unable to see but believed was there. When Paul said that "we were in slavery," he could have been combining both of these beliefs, or he could have been using an editorial "we." (For example, in 1 Corinthians 10:1 Paul referred to "our forefathers," which obviously would not have included the Corinthians.) Paul's thrust in this section is the oppression of slavery.

Even though the situation looked bad and the outlook even worse, Paul declared, "But when the time had fully come, God sent his Son, born of a woman, born under law, to redeem those under law, that we might receive the full rights of sons" (4:4-5). God chose the exact time in history to send the once-and-for-all sacrifice. History approves of God's timetable. The *Pax Romana* (Roman Peace) began with Octavius Caesar Augustus in 17 B.C. (Luke 2:2) and lasted until A.D. 180. The characteristics of this era included peace throughout the empire (even though social unrest doesn't stop the spread of the gospel), a common culture that helped in cross-cultural communication, common languages, protection by Roman law, a vast network of roads, and a stable economy. Old religions were dying out, and the people were beginning to realize that old philosophies were powerless to change men.

Jesus was human (born of a woman) and understood the judgments of law (born under law). His purpose for coming to earth was to redeem man or to set him free by paying a price for him (3:13). In the first century, you could buy a slave and either keep him or set him free. The message for the Galatians was simple: Jesus had bought them from the slavery of the law; to return to slavery was unthinkable! To return to slavery when you have been redeemed is to totally undo Christ's work at the cross. If the Galatians—or you—bought a gospel of slavery, then Christ died for nothing (2:21).

Because the Galatians had bought this different gospel, they were no longer sons (3:26) but had become slaves. It's far better to be a son than a slave. Why? "Because you are sons, God sent the Spirit of his Son into our hearts, the Spirit who calls out, 'Abba, Father' " (4:6). As a full-fledged son, you have the Spirit of His Son, which calls out, "Abba, Father." The Spirit in the believer's life is a right of sonship. A slave can't address his master with such endearing terms as "Abba, Father," but the son can. Paul urged the Galatians to look closely at what was happening to them—they were opting for slavery over sonship! How absurd can you be!

"Abba, Father" denotes the closeness of a child to the Father. Jesus used this phrase in communing with

His Father (Mark 14:36). The Spirit isn't sent into our hearts to make us sons; the Spirit is sent because we are already sons (Acts 2:38; 5:32). Paul testified to this truth in Romans 8:15: "For you did not receive a spirit that makes you a slave again to fear, but you received the Spirit of sonship. And by him we cry, 'Abba, Father.' " Paul declared they were not slaves to fear (a works-righteousness always produces a fear of never doing enough) but were recipients of His Spirit, which cries, "Abba, Father." Romans 8:16 is similar to Galatians 4:6: "The Spirit himself testifies with our spirit that we are God's children." In Romans 8:15, we cry, "Abba, Father," while in Galatians 4:6, the Spirit cries, "Abba, Father"; hence, they testify to each other (Romans 8:16). They are saying the same thing.

What is the conclusion of this illustration in 4:1-6? "So you are no longer a slave, but a son; and since you are a son, God has made you also an heir" (4:7). Paul's desire for the Galatians was for them to accept sonship and not to opt for any kind of slavery ever again! When the advantages of sonship over slavery are compared, the decision should be obvious. The son has the same nature as the father, but the servant does not. The son will always be a member of the family, even if he makes a mistake, but if the servant makes a mistake, he could be sent away. The son has a father while the servant has a master. The son obeys out of love while the slave obeys out of fear. The son has a future (Luke 15:18-19), while the servant has none.

Being a slave isn't desirable. A slave receives little or no wages, has no days off, receives no hospitalization or other insurance, and has no retirement. However, the Judaizers knew they could get more work and productivity from slaves than from free sons. If productivity is the standard for the right gospel, man must return to slavery! Returning to slavery is considered to be negative. "This matter arose because some false brothers had infiltrated our ranks to spy on the freedom we have in Christ Jesus and to make us slaves" (2:4). "But now that you know God—or rather are known by God—how is that you are turning back to those weak and miserable principles? Do you wish to be enslaved by them all over again?" (4:9). The productivity of this "different gospel" appealed to some and even gave credibility to the Judaizers, but Paul, in no uncertain terms, condemned it (1:6-10)! To boast that a gospel is from God because of its productivity is to agree with Paul's opponents. Paul wasn't about to reason that if it wasn't from God, it would come to nothing (see Acts 5:39). If that reasoning were true, it lends credibility and sanction to world religions (such as Islam) and cults (Mormonism and Jehovah's Witnesses). Productivity and perpetual existence can't be proofs of rightness. Every modern gospel must be measured by the ancient gospel. If your religion is one of bondage, slavery, fear, anxiety, and guilt, Paul would say, what gospel do you have?

Jesus contrasted slavery with sonship: "I tell you the truth, everyone who sins is a slave to sin. Now a slave has no permanent place in the family, but a son belongs to it forever. So if the Son sets you free, you will be free indeed" (John 8:34-36). Paul said that faith is the channel to sonship (3:26). The son is accepted by the Father who meets his needs and calms his fears. Rejecting sonship for slavery made no sense to Paul and left him "astonished" (1:6) and "perplexed" (4:20). Perhaps a low self-image and a misunderstanding of God made slavery an option. The "prodigal" son didn't see himself as a returning son; he thought he should be classed among the slaves (Luke 15:19). His father's willingness to treat him as a full-fledged son shows the nature of God's grace and love. "But the father said to his servants, 'Quick! Bring the best robe and put it on him. Put a ring on his finger and sandals on his feet. Bring the fattened calf and kill it. Let's have a feast and celebrate. For this son of mine was dead and is alive again; he was lost and is found' " (Luke 15:22-24).

Please observe that even though Paul realized that Christians are children of God (4:7), he viewed himself as a slave (Romans 1:1; 1 Corinthians 9:19) in his behavior, which was a response to his sonship/adoption by God.

2. Paul rebuked their regression (4:8-11). Paul became very emotional in arguing for adoption as sons as being far superior to any slavery, past or present. He began by summarizing the Galatians' past: "Formerly, when you did not know God, you were slaves to those who by nature are not gods" (4:8). He referred to the time before their conversion when they had no knowledge of the true God (Acts 14:8-20) and worshiped idols, which has always been condemned by God (Exodus 20:3-4; Isaiah 44:6-20; Jeremiah 2:26-29; 10:1-5). He also reminded them of their slave state before their conversion (4:3).

Paul left his polemic platform and confronted them with where they were at that very moment: "But now that you know God—or rather are known by God—how is it that you are turning back to those weak and miserable principles?" (4:9a). "Knowing God" refers to being sons and heirs in this new relationship. The phrase "rather are known by God" communicates God's initiative in establishing the relationship. Paul couldn't understand how they could leave this new relationship! "You are turning" indicated they were still in the process. They were turning back to "weak and miserable principles," which is an allusion to the "basic principles of the world" (4:3). They were weak because they were powerless to establish a relationship with God. *Miserable* means to "crouch or cower," i.e., to fear, and fear was the outstanding characteristic of paganism or legalism.

How they could have regressed to this "different gospel" with all its negative trappings was beyond Paul's understanding. He raised a question they had to answer: "Do you wish to be enslaved by them all over again?" (4:9b). This question shows they had been enslaved once (4:3) but had experienced freedom (4:31; 5:1, 13). Granted, it wasn't the same slavery they had come out of, but what difference did that make? It was still slavery! His question indicates that his work with these churches had been destroyed. Using "again" in the question and in other places (4:19; 5:1) marks the extent of their regression.

The nature of their "new slavery" had a definite Jewish tint. "You are observing special days and months and seasons and years!" (4:10). Paul wasn't opposed to observing special days (1 Corinthians 16:8) any more than he was opposed to circumcision (Acts 16:3), but he *never* considered them a part of a works-righteousness, human-merit religion! No human work can claim to be redemptive and at the same time declare the all-sufficiency of the cross to save. With this type of religion (4:10), a dreary, burdensome routine develops, resulting in a total falling away from God (5:4). Paul's greatest fear was that he had wasted his efforts on them: "I fear for you, that somehow I have wasted my efforts on you" (4:11).

This rebuke in 4:8-11 came at the end of Paul's argument on the advantages of sonship over slavery. His emotions are obvious. You can see his deep concern over the situation. He knew the ultimate outcome of accepting a different gospel—despair, depression, guilt, anxiety, and eventual destruction (6:8). This new gospel was "bad news." Granted, it sounded like the "good news" that Paul preached, but the differences (not the similarities) spelled destruction for all who accepted it. This is the inherent danger in false teaching—it usually isn't totally wrong, but the differences are wrong. Even though the Galatians were young Christians, it was their choice to accept the different gospel (note the use of "let yourselves" in 5:1-2 as an example of their choosing).

Paul's attitude toward the false teachers who had led the Galatians astray is equally clear (1:8-9; 5:10, 12). He didn't view the false teachers' work among the Galatians as just a difference in approach; he perceived a difference in the essence and content of the real gospel. Paul allowed a personal difference between brothers, such as he had with Barnabas (Acts 15:39), to go unattacked; but when the difference pertained to the work of Christ on the cross, there could be no compromise or variation without someone being an enemy of the cross (Philippians 3:18).

E. Argument from Relationship (4:12-20)

With his pen still warm from his strong rebuke, Paul now argued from the viewpoint of the love the Galatians had for him and his love for them.

1. The Galatians' affection for Paul (4:12-16). The plea based on their relationship becomes clear in 4:12: "I plead with you, brothers, become like me, for I became like you. You have done me no wrong." He was pleading for his brothers to be like him because he had sought to be like them (1 Corinthians 9:22). He wanted them to have the same freedom that he had.

Paul told why he had preached to the Galatians and how they had received him: "As you know, it was because of an illness that I first preached the gospel to you. Even though my illness was a trial to you, you did not treat me with contempt or scorn. Instead, you welcomed me as if I were an angel of God, as if I were Christ Jesus himself" (4:13-14). The reference to Paul's illness is too vague to determine. It is believed that he contracted malaria in the lowlands of Pamphylia and went to the cooler mountain region of Galatia to recuperate. While he was recovering, he took the opportunity to preach the gospel to them. Many ancient people considered illness as a punishment for an evil deed. However, the Galatians didn't treat Paul with contempt or scorn; they felt he was an angel of God.

Paul realized that the Galatians were now missing an essential characteristic in the Christian life, so he simply posed the probing question: "What has happened to all your joy?" (4:15a). He was saying, "I remember how you were. What happened?" True righteousness produces joy because it comes from God; hence, it isn't a product of the Christian's effort. The Galatians had bought a gospel from the Judaizers based on what man did rather than on what God had done. When joy stems from performance, you are happy only when you perform well. For example, you are happy when you get four hits out of four trips at bat. How do you feel when you strike out? Joy that is based on a good performance is temporary because eventually there will be a bad performance. If you need a "because of" to document your salvation, let it be "because of" something God does.

The Galatians' affection for Paul was so strong that they would have sacrificed anything for him—even their very eyes. "I can testify that, if you could have

99

done so, you would have torn out your eyes and given them to me" (4:15b). Because of their relationship, they shouldn't have considered Paul an enemy for sharing the truth with them. "Have I now become your enemy by telling you the truth?" (4:16).

2. Paul's affection for them (4:17-20). Paul referred to the false brothers (2:4) as "those people" when he questioned their motives for being involved with the Galatian Christians: "Those people are zealous to win you over, but for no good. What they want is to alienate you from us, so that you may be zealous for them" (4:17). The false teachers were trying to alienate Paul's converts and were trying to get them zealous for them. Paul never sought for men to become "Paulites" (1 Corinthians 1:12), but the false teachers wanted to boast in their followers (6:12-13). Paul's attitude toward his converts was different from that of the false teachers toward their "converts." The real difference between the two approaches is the difference between grace (freedom) and legalism (slavery).

When Christianity is seen as freedom in Christ (which it is), Christians are not in subservience to their human teachers, because their ambition is to become mature in Christ. But when Christianity is turned into a bondage to rules and regulations, its victims are inevitably in subjection, tied to the apron-strings of their teacher, as in the Middle Ages.[1]

Paul wasn't opposed to zeal for the proper purpose. "It is fine to be zealous, provided the purpose is good, and to be so always and not just when I am with you" (4:18).

Paul's love for the Galatians is evident as he brings the relationship argument to an end. "My dear

---

[1]Stott, p. 116.

children, for whom I am again in the pains of childbirth until Christ is formed in you, how I wish I could be with you now and change my tone, because I am perplexed about you!" (4:19-20). "My dear children," an expression that Paul used only once, conveyed his love for and attitude toward them. He would willingly go through the "pains of childbirth" a second time for the same child. What love! "Again" indicates that the first birth was aborted because Christ was no longer in them. Paul saw the dynamic for conduct coming from Christ within rather than from a yoke without. Paul didn't want Christ to simply dwell within them; he wanted Christ to be formed in them (Colossians 1:27). The goal for all preachers should be to help form Christ in every convert.

Paul closed this section by expressing his desire to be with them because of his great concern for them. Because the Galatians were Paul's spiritual children, his love for them could be compared to a mother's love. He didn't believe the false teachers' concern for the Galatians was as deep as his. "The difference between Paul and the false teachers should now be clear. The false teachers were seeking themselves to dominate the Galatians; Paul longed that Christ be formed in them. They had a selfish eye to their own prestige and position; Paul was prepared to sacrifice himself for them, to be in travail until Christ was formed in them."[2]

F. Argument from an Allegory (4:21-31)

Paul's final argument in the defense of the gospel of salvation by grace is an allegory. An allegory takes

---

[2]Stott, pp. 116-17.

a historical event and presents a parallel truth. It is very similar to the type and antitype analogies found in the book of Hebrews. However, this is the only allegory found in the New Testament.

Paul had already determined his beliefs and merely adapted them to the story of Abraham and Sarah. He wasn't saying that Abraham and Sarah's story taught that his theology was correct; he used it as an illustration. It is irresponsible to build belief by allegorizing or spiritualizing a text without determining the soundness of the position from the Word of God. The early church went into apostasy mainly by allegorizing the Bible and proof-texting their religion on unrelated passages. The religious world has taught untold errors in this manner in spite of quoting book, chapter, and verse. For example, rebuilding the walls of Jerusalem or Joshua's walking around the walls of Jericho has nothing to do with the twentieth-century church today. Although we can learn many truths from the Old Testament stories (Romans 15:4; 1 Corinthians 10:11), we should never build a new belief or teaching for the twentieth-century church from them. If this method (allegory) becomes the means of discovering truth through "progressive revelation," you can never test your truth or challenge anyone else's "discovery." Paul used it because he was inspired and had a direct revelation (1:12). Responsible Bible study isn't based on allegory or adapting passages to fit a practice.

An allegory is sometimes referred to as a "prolonged metaphor." Allegories were developed in the sixth century B.C. in Greece "to remove anthropomorphisms and crude literalisms which offended the Greek mind. . . . Jerome is chiefly responsible for introducing allegory into the Roman church and this subsequently became one of the great issues of the Reformation.

Luther, Melanchthon and Calvin rejected allegory because it is subjective and controlled."[3]

Philo of Alexandria (20 B.C.–A.D. 42) was a strong advocate of using this method of biblical interpretation. It was adopted by the early church fathers and is still defended and practiced by the present-day Catholic church. In preaching, this method allows one to draw spiritual truths from historical statements and thus make an application never intended by the writer. One example of this is seen when allegorizing the story of the Exodus. Egypt could represent the temptations and allurements of sin (Hebrews 11:15). Salvation from death and destruction was provided for by a lamb, which could represent Jesus (John 1:29). Because of the blood of the lamb, the Israelites were saved from destruction.

On that same night I will pass through Egypt and strike down every firstborn—both men and animals—and I will bring judgment on all the gods of Egypt. I am the LORD. The blood will be a sign for you on the houses where you are; and when I see the blood, I will pass over you. No destructive plague will touch you when I strike Egypt (Exodus 12:12-13).

After the Israelites were saved by the blood of the lamb (as we are saved or freed by the blood [Revelation 1:5]), they were baptized in the Red Sea. "For I do not want you to be ignorant of the fact, brothers, that our forefathers were all under the cloud and that they all passed through the sea. They were all baptized into Moses in the cloud and in the sea" (1 Corinthians 10:1-2). Allegorizing the facts of the Exodus story could teach that men are saved by the blood of Jesus without

[3]David H. Wallace, "Allegory," in *Baker's Dictionary of Theology* (Grand Rapids: Baker Book House, 1960), pp. 36-37.

103

baptism, which isn't true according to other plain teachings (Mark 16:15-16; Acts 2:38; 22:16; Romans 6:3-4; 1 Peter 3:21). Using the Exodus story this way is a classic illustration of deciding what you believe *before* looking at Scripture, then finding a story to fit that belief. Allegory can be used to justify any action or conduct.

1. Historical facts of the allegory (4:21-23). Paul introduced this section by addressing the readers who had opted for the law: "Tell me, you who want to be under the law, are you not aware of what the law says?" (4:21).

Paul set up his allegory by giving the facts of the story. His stress is on the two sons because of their different origins. One son came in the ordinary manner (after the flesh) whereas the other was a result of the promise. "For it is written that Abraham had two sons, one by the slave woman and the other by the free woman. His son by the slave woman was born in the ordinary way; but his son by the free woman was born as the result of a promise" (4:22-23).

2. Interpreting the facts of the allegory (4:24-27). These things may be taken figuratively, for the women represent two covenants. One covenant is from Mount Sinai and bears children who are to be slaves: This is Hagar. Now Hagar stands for Mount Sinai in Arabia and corresponds to the present city of Jerusalem, because she is in slavery with her children. But the Jerusalem that is above is free, and she is our mother. For it is written:

"Be glad, O barren woman,
    who bears no children;
break forth and cry aloud,
    you who have no labor pains;
because more are the children of the desolate woman
    than of her who has a husband" (4:24-27).

Paul's contrast can best be seen in the following analysis:

Hagar (slave)	Sarah (free)
Law	Grace
Ishmael (child after flesh)	Isaac (son of promise)
Flesh	Spirit
Old Covenant	New Covenant
Earthly Jerusalem	Heavenly Jerusalem
Slaves Under Law	Free Under Grace

3. Applying the allegory to the readers (4:28-30). This application began with the salutation of "brothers" and told the Galatians that they were children of promise (3:29). "Now you, brothers, like Isaac, are children of promise" (4:28).

Paul spoke of the persecution of the church by referring to Ishmael's persecution of Isaac. "At that time the son born in the ordinary way persecuted the son born by the power of the Spirit. It is the same now" (4:29). There is no record of Ishmael's persecution of Isaac in the Genesis account, but it could be a reference to later persecution of the Israelites (Isaac's descendants) by some of Ishmael's descendants (Judges 8:24; Psalm 83:5-6). The churches of Galatia had known about persecution when the gospel was first preached in their area (Acts 13:50; 14:2-5, 19).

Paul declared that either justification by faith (promise) or justification by law-keeping (flesh) had to go—they couldn't coexist. "But what does the Scripture say? 'Get rid of the slave woman and her son, for the slave woman's son will never share in the inheritance with the free woman's son' " (4:30).

4. Concluding the allegory (4:31). In concluding the allegory, Paul drove home his point by saying "therefore, brothers." His statement following the preface is the whole point of the allegory. "Therefore, brothers, we are not children of the slave woman, but of the free woman" (4:31). To revert to a system of slavery was foolishness to Paul. His allegory was constructed to show their erroneous reasoning. Salvation by grace is superior in every form.

The first covenant was announced at a physical mount; the new covenant at a spiritual peak in man's history. When the first was announced, those who heard it were cautioned not to draw near or to cross a boundary. When the second was given, they were invited to "Draw near with a true heart in full assurance" (Hebrews 10:22). The first was engraved upon stone, and was as inflexible as the material upon which it was carved. The second was written upon the hearts of believers, and was as warm as the faith that led them to receive Jesus. The first bound the recipients to God upon the threat that the iniquities of the fathers would be visited upon the children to the third and fourth generations. The second drew the respondents by the promise that their sins would be remembered no more forever. Truly it is a "better covenant, based upon better promises!"[4]

Paul presented six arguments in support of his gospel of salvation by grace. If his readers listened to the letter with great care, they couldn't help believing the truth (4:16). Why, in every generation, does the church have its own group of Pharisees? Because people want them! Some people love the security of walls and gun towers rather than freedom. The Gentile Christians had a natural attraction to Jewish legalism because they had come from a system that sought to please all gods, even the "unknown god" (Acts 17:23).

Paul's message was so simple that those who had come out of a slavery to pagan gods could understand

[4]W. Carl Ketcherside, *A Study of the Covenants* (Cassville, Mo.: Litho Printers), p. 94.

it. Doing works of merit for these gods was so much a part of their emotional makeup that it was hard to change and simply accept a gospel of grace. It wasn't Paul's fault that the Galatians didn't accept his logical and heartfelt arguments. The sway and control of the false teachers over the lives of the members of the Galatian churches overshadowed their intellect and kept them in emotional bondage to the false teachers (4:17). The Galatian letter shows the difficulty of emotionally accepting what the intellect says is true. The gospel of grace is so divine and so unnatural that it's difficult for men to accept it as truth because, in reality, it's too good to be true!

Application for Today

God has always sought to be with His people. God is the Father (4:2), and His children are made in His image (Genesis 1:26). God's acceptance of us is demonstrated by the gift of the Spirit of His Son. "Because you are sons, God sent the Spirit of his Son into our hearts, the Spirit who calls out, 'Abba, Father' " (4:6). Being accepted by God as sons grants us the opportunity to "receive the full rights of sons" (4:5), and one of those rights is the opportunity to have such a close relationship with God that He can be addressed as "Abba" (see Romans 8:15).

Our closeness to God enables us to see Him as our Father, not as an employer or a policeman. We do not have to work to gain the presence of God because God, as our Father, is always present. "For it is God who works in you to will and to act according to his good purpose" (Philippians 2:13). We must live in harmony with His presence. Being aware that we are always in the presence of God can be a great motivator

for godly living. Just as we were careful to behave in
the presence of our earthly father, we should also
behave carefully in the presence of our heavenly
Father.

To aid the Christian in feeling comfortable in
approaching Him, God has provided an excellent high
priest who understands the temptations and struggles
of being in human flesh.

Therefore, since we have a great high priest who has gone
through the heavens, Jesus the Son of God, let us hold
firmly to the faith we profess. For we do not have a high
priest who is unable to sympathize with our weaknesses,
but we have one who has been tempted in every way, just
as we are—yet was without sin. Let us then approach the
throne of grace with confidence, so that we may receive
mercy and find grace (Hebrews 4:14-16).

The Galatians had a special place in Paul's heart.
He saw them as his "brothers" (4:12) and his "dear
children" (4:19). One of the great needs in today's
church is for Christians to have close relationships with
other Christians.

In order to have the relationship between Christians
that God desires, several factors must be present. A
very important one would be a willingness to suffer
or be inconvenienced for another Christian. The
Galatians and Paul had that type of relationship: "I can
testify that, if you could have done so, you would have
torn out your eyes and given them to me" (4:15b).
Sacrificing for one another draws people together. A
community that responds to a local disaster develops
a close relationship.

Being involved in the lives of other Christians is
really not an option. "If one part suffers, every part
suffers with it; if one part is honored, every part

rejoices with it" (1 Corinthians 12:26). The Christian must ask, Does my relationship with others stop awt the point of personal sacrifice and inconvenience?

A second factor in building relationships is truthfulness. "Have I now become your enemy by telling you the truth?" (4:16). It wasn't easy for Paul to confront the Galatians with their acceptance of another gospel. He did not delight in referring to them as "foolish Galatians" (3:1). Nor was it easy for Paul to speak the truth to Peter about his actions (2:11-14). The truth should always be spoken in love (Ephesians 4:15). Do we encourage relationships where we are told what we *want* to hear or what we *need* to hear? Do we want relationships that rubber-stamp our ideas and actions, or those that are objective and honest?

Third, the relationship should fulfill the purpose for all Christians—to have Christ formed in us (4:19). Paul viewed Christ's being in the Christian as part of the plan of God. "To them God has chosen to make known among the Gentiles the glorious riches of this mystery, which is Christ in you, the hope of glory" (Colossians 1:27). What are the purposes of your relationships with Christians? Are they purely social, or do they have spiritual ends?

When the Christian develops a closeness with God, he will desire to have a closeness with the people of God. Just as it was expensive for God to be close to us (John 3:16), so will it be expensive for us to be close to one another. "Be devoted to one another in brotherly love" (Romans 12:10a).

Thought Questions for Chapter Nine

1. What part does the Spirit play in the life of the Christian? (See Romans 8.)

2. How can deep and abiding relationships be formed with other Christians?
3. What does it mean to have Christ formed in us?
4. How can Christians develop a greater Christ-centered life?
5. What are some ways that Christians can communicate their concern for others?

CHAPTER
TEN

LIFE OF LIBERTY
—PART I

A. Life of Freedom (5:1-15)

Paul turns from argument to application, from the doctrinal to the practical. The Christian who lives by faith is not going to become a rebel. Quite the contrary, he is going to experience the inner discipline of God that is far better than the outer discipline of man-made rules. No man could become a rebel who depends on God's grace, yields to God's spirit, lives for others, and seeks to glorify God. The legalist is the one who eventually rebels, because he is living in bondage, depending on the flesh, living for self, and seeking the praise of men and not the glory of God.

No, Paul's doctrine of Christian liberty through grace is not the dangerous doctrine. It is legalism that is the dangerous doctrine, because legalism attempts to do the impossible: change the old nature and make it obey the laws of God. Legalism succeeds for a short time, and then the flesh begins to rebel. The surrendered Christian who depends on the power of the Spirit is not denying the law of God, or rebelling against it. Rather, that law is being fulfilled in him through the Spirit (Romans 8:1-4).[1]

1. Freedom versus legalism (5:1-6). The thoughts in these opening verses are tied to the closing thoughts

---

[1]Warren W. Wiersbe, *Be Free: Galatians* (SP Publications, 1975), pp. 113-14.

of the previous chapter. The declaration was made that Christians' roots are in the free woman (4:31). Jesus is the One who set man free; man was a prisoner of sin (3:22) and law (3:23) before Christ did His work. The freedom found in Jesus is both *from* and *to*. It is a freedom *from* the guilt and reign of sin (Romans 6:17-18) and the constant, unsuccessful attempt to keep the law in order to win God's favor. It is a freedom *to* live without sin's control, to love one another (5:13-14), and to experience the joy of justification and adoption. Jesus taught this great truth in His ministry: "I tell you the truth, everyone who sins is a slave to sin. Now a slave has no permanent place in the family, but a son belongs to it forever. So if the Son sets you free, you will be free indeed" (John 8:34-36). Human courts can justify (render the accused guiltless), but the judge doesn't adopt the accused and make him a part of his family with full rights of sonship. However, spiritually, God forgives and adopts the accused in one complete motion. Our forgiveness, a simple judicial decision, is the result of a God who wants us not only to be pardoned but to be *His*!

Paul used three comparisons to explain the fallacy of trusting law as a redemptive means for salvation, and all three have a negative connotation. The first comparison was the "child-leader" who was to serve as a guardian to keep man under the care and direction of another with little or no freedom (translated "put in charge to lead," and "supervision" [3:24, 25]). The second comparison was the slave woman (4:22, 30-31). If you could choose to be like a mother and son, you wouldn't select Hagar and Ishmael; you would choose Sarah and Isaac who were free. The third comparison was a yoke. The Jewish nation had been enslaved to foreign powers for most of the past seven hundred years. Their forefathers had felt the yoke of Egyptian slavery (Leviticus 26:13), and since the time of the literary prophets, the Jews had worn the yokes of the Assyrians, Babylonians, and Romans. The Jews didn't like to be reminded of their slavery and even tried to forget it. When Jesus taught about the truth setting men free (John 8:32), the Jews had a quick answer: "We are Abraham's descendants and have *never* been slaves of anyone" (John 8:33, emphasis added). Consequently, the comparison of the yoke carried a bad connotation.

Based on the freedom that Jesus brought to all Christians, Paul urged his readers to "stand firm" and not to return to any form of slavery. Prior to their conversion, the Galatians had been burdened ("held in") by a yoke, and it was Paul's desire that this not happen "again." A yoke was used to get oxen to perform and produce work that they would not willingly do if they were free. The yoke of the law was unbearable for those who had grown up subjected to it (Acts 15:10); hence, the Gentiles who had grown up without it didn't stand a chance to conform to it. The yoke of the law offered a "quick fix" in producing behavioral changes and in ceasing from life-dominating sins.

The changes were immediate, visual, and radical, but Paul knew from history and experience (Romans 7:12-15) that something else was required to be successful over the long haul. The outward, fleshly actions can be controlled only so long by law, for if the "want to's" aren't dealt with, a real transformation won't occur. For example, changes in diet are good, but the appetite must also be changed, focused, and rechanneled if there is to be a permanent weight loss. The yoke of law will make a person "sit down" on the outside while he is "standing up" on the inside.

There is more to the Christian life than behavioral changes. A person can be trained to act like a Christian without ever being a Christian. This "acting" can have its dynamic in a yoke that puts the untrained under the direction of a leader, or the untrained can be yoked with the trained and perform identically. Only without the yoke can you ascertain if the inner man has truly been changed. A Christianity that produced slavery to the law was foreign to Paul's understanding. Christian behavior that is orchestrated from an inner restraint will be successful, regardless of circumstances. Guidelines are good while the Spirit is in the process of taking over the flesh (5:16, 25), but lasting, joyous Christian conduct must flow as a result of Christ being formed within the Christian (2:20; 4:19).

With the assertion that freedom is found only in Jesus and the accompanying warning against returning to slavery, Paul explained the danger of abandoning faith in the work of Christ for faith in man's ability to perform redemptive works (5:2-4). Paul's emotions are again revealed in the use of phrases such as, "Mark my words! I, Paul . . . ," and "Again I declare. . . ." If the Galatians accepted circumcision (circumcision isn't a single act but represents the principle of a works-righteousness system), four results would naturally follow. First, "Christ will be of no value to you at all" (5:2b). Christ is valuable only to those who realize that they can't save themselves and must depend on the grace of God.

A second result of accepting circumcision would be the individual's obligation to obey all the law. "Again I declare to every man who lets himself be circumcised that he is obligated to obey the whole law" (5:3). Apparently, the false teachers didn't necessarily want the Galatians to obey the whole law; but if they

114

accepted part of the law, logic would demand obedience to all the law.

A third result of accepting circumcision would be alienation from Christ. "You who are trying to be justified by law have been alienated from Christ" (5:4a). When humans try to supplement Christ's work, they lose their relationship with Christ. Christ can't share in a gospel based on human effort and works of righteousness.

A fourth result would be falling "away from grace" (5:4b). When the Christian proclaims that he can't save himself but then obeys circumcision, he's guilty of open contradiction. Obedience to a gospel of human effort brings about separation from grace, and grace is really the only means by which man has ever been saved.

There are two ways for man to be lost. One is to follow a life-style of rebellion against the will and ways of God (1 Samuel 15:23). Another is to try to save himself, which is an insult to God.

Paul's readers should now have an understanding of the dangers of legalism. The Galatians not only had bought an additional religious policy but also had lost the insurance they had gained from Paul's gospel of grace. Paul now switched from the negative to the positive and told the Galatians what Christians expect: "For we through the Spirit, by faith, are waiting for the hope of righteousness" (5:5, NASV). Note that Paul changed from "you" to "we." He declared that by faith (not works) we eagerly wait (not work) through the Spirit (not flesh) for the righteousness we hope. Paul's hope wasn't wishful thinking but honest expectation.

In two places in the letter, Paul made summary statements, attempting to put the whole book in one verse: "For in Christ Jesus neither circumcision nor uncircumcision has any value. The only thing that counts is faith expressing itself through love" (5:6); and "Neither circumcision nor uncircumcision means anything; what counts is a new creation" (6:15). Circumcision doesn't improve or diminish our standing with God; all that matters is an expressive faith.

2. *Warning against false teachers (5:7-12).* In these verses, Paul switched from "we" to "you." "You were running a good race. Who cut in on you and kept you from obeying the truth?" (5:7). (It wasn't unusual for Paul to use athletic metaphors in his writings; see 1 Corinthians 9:24-27; 2 Timothy 4:6-8). Someone came from off the track and had "cut in" on their race. These outside forces had stopped them from obeying the truth (2:5, 14; 4:16).

For the benefit of the Galatians, Paul described the false teachers who had created the problem for them.

a) Origin. "That kind of persuasion does not come from the one who calls you" (5:8). The false teachers' message wasn't the one the Galatians had received in the beginning (1:6).

b) Effect. "A little yeast works through the whole batch of dough" (5:9). This different gospel was spreading. Apparently, a large number of people were accepting the false gospel, and its influence was growing. Paul wasn't impressed with its popular appeal and used a common object (yeast) to describe the false teaching. He used the same idea elsewhere and referred to it as evil (1 Corinthians 5:6).

c) End. "I am confident in the Lord that you will take no other view. The one who is throwing you into confusion will pay the penalty, whoever he may be" (5:10). Earlier, Paul had alluded to the confusion created by the false teachers (1:7). He was convinced that God would take care of the teachers who had done such destructive work among the Galatian churches.

116

Paul ended this section with a plea for himself and a wish for his opponents: "Brothers, if I am still preaching circumcision, why am I still being persecuted? In that case, the offense of the cross has been abolished. As for those agitators, I wish they would go the whole way and emasculate themselves!" (5:11-12). Paul used a rhetorical question that implied that his opponents were accusing him of preaching circumcision (perhaps they were using Acts 16:3 as proof). He reasoned that if this was true, why was he still being opposed (persecuted)? If what they were saying was true, the offense of the cross (can't be saved by any human effort) was eliminated.

Paul had addressed his opponents as "those people" (4:17) and "one who is throwing you into confusion" (5:10), and here he added a new description, "those agitators" (5:12). Because of Paul's great love for the Galatians (4:19) and his strong hatred for false teaching (1:6-9), he wished that the knife would slip and the false teachers would emasculate ("mutilate," NASV) themselves. (According to Deuteronomy 23:1, such a person would not be allowed in the assembly of the Lord.) This verse shows the seriousness of the false gospel and Paul's opposition against it. The following summarizes Paul's attitude toward false teachers:

Thus Paul set himself and the false teachers in stark contrast. They were preaching circumcision; he was preaching Christ and the cross. To preach circumcision is to tell sinners that they can save themselves by their own good works; to preach Christ crucified is to tell them that they cannot and that only Christ can save them through the cross. The message of circumcision is quite inoffensive, popular because flattering; the message of Christ crucified is, however, offensive to human pride, unpopular because unflattering. So to preach circumcision is to avoid persecution; to preach Christ crucified is to invite it. People hate to be told that they can be saved only at the foot of the cross, and they oppose the preacher who tells them so.

Now since he was being persecuted, Paul argues that he was not preaching circumcision. On the contrary, he was preaching Christ crucified, and the stumbling-block of the cross had not been removed. It was the false teachers who were pressing the Galatians to be circumcised, in order to avoid persecution for the cross of Christ (see Galatians 6:12).[2]

3. What Christian freedom is not (5:13-15). Paul's declaration to freedom is clear: "You, my brothers, were called to be free." However, your Christian liberty shouldn't be viewed as your achievement. You didn't escape from prison (3:22-23) but were rescued (1:4) and liberated by Jesus. You didn't tear away the yoke of legalism; it was lifted by God. Paul's opposition to the slavery of a law-keeping system and his commendation of sonship with its resulting freedom have been clear since 2:4. Yet, he was afraid that the freedom his gospel proclaimed could be abused if the freedom of grace was misunderstood. (See Romans 6:1 and Jude 4 for examples of abused freedom.) Since Paul didn't want his young converts to end up with a misguided freedom, he explained what is *not* included in Christian freedom.

a) Freedom doesn't allow you opportunity to indulge in your fleshly desires. "You, my brothers, were called to be free. But do not use your freedom to indulge the sinful nature" (5:13a). "Indulge" is used to denote a base of operations for a war (Romans 7:8, 11; 2 Corinthians 5:12; 11:12; 1 Timothy 5:14). It has been translated as an "opportunity for the flesh" (NASV).

---

[2]Stott, pp. 136-37.

b) Freedom doesn't grant you the privilege of injuring a brother. "Rather, serve one another in love" (5:13b). When you adopt an attitude of loving service to your fellow Christians, you can't harm your brother. Dissension is the antithesis of service. "If you keep on biting and devouring each other, watch out or you will be destroyed by each other" (5:15). If biting and devouring (present tense indicating the actions were still taking place) continued, the end result would be destruction. Because the Galatians had accepted the human-effort gospel, their focus was now on the flesh. A fleshly oriented religion leads to fleshly sins. There is an ancient Greek myth describing a snake fight; a snake grabbed another one by the tail and swallowed it. Possibly this could be the allusion found in 5:15.

c) Freedom doesn't approve a disregard for the law. "The entire law is summed up in a single command: 'Love your neighbor as yourself' " (5:14). This command has been taught throughout the Scriptures (see Leviticus 19:18; Matthew 5:43; 22:39; James 2:8). Referring to the "entire law" is not uncommon in the New Testament (Galatians 5:3; James 2:10). Paul also wrote about carrying burdens that will result in fulfilling the "law of Christ" (Galatians 6:2). The law of Christ involves loving your neighbors (Luke 10:25-37).

Two great dangers facing the church in every generation are legalism on the one hand and license (thinking you can do whatever you want) on the other. It is strange that these two extremes claim the same source. Neither extreme will ever be evangelistic. Legalism produces a church that feels it must be right on "ten thousand" different points of doctrine, so all efforts are devoted to keeping the flock convinced and reassured about the "ten thousand" points. The other extreme produces a church with no distinctiveness and

119

no vital message because everything is "relative." Paul didn't want the Galatians to reject legalism and to embrace grace to the extent that grace would be used as a license for any type of conduct.

Christianity must never be seen as a culture or tradition. It's possible for an individual to be religious and traditional without being a disciple of Jesus! Christianity is a way of life but the way of life focused in Jesus (John 14:6).

B. Life Controlled by the Spirit (5:16-26)

When Paul wrote about the doctrine of liberty, he warned about two extreme reactions: bondage (5:1) and license (5:13).

1. Christians should walk by the Spirit (5:16-18). You shouldn't reason that there are no standards under grace. Grace is freedom to do as the "one who called you"—God Himself (1:6; 5:8)—not as you will. A life controlled by the Spirit opposes a life with a focus on the flesh. "So I say, live by the Spirit, and you will not gratify the desires of the sinful nature. For the sinful nature desires what is contrary to the Spirit, and the Spirit what is contrary to the sinful nature. They are in conflict with each other, so that you do not do what you want" (5:16-17).

The flesh and the Spirit are enemies and in continual conflict. You will always have to make a conscious effort to choose God's way (1 Corinthians 9:24-27). Paul linked the Spirit with living (5:16, 25) and being led (5:18). Being directed by the Spirit doesn't involve an outward restraint (law). "But if you are led by the Spirit, you are not under law" (5:18). Change requires an inner restraint rather than a dependence on an outward force.

2. Works of the flesh (5:19-21). Paul's purpose in contrasting the works of the flesh with the fruit of the Spirit was to illustrate the end result of living by the gospel his opponents preached as opposed to the gospel he preached. The false gospel centered on human merit and fleshly achievements; therefore, those who focused on the flesh would evidence it in their ungodly ways. Those who focused on the Spirit (5:16, 18, 25) would show His fruit produced in their lives. A religion of law concentrating on fleshly control will eventually fail because long-term behavioral changes will be affected only by a transformation from within ("Christ in you" [4:19; Colossians 1:27]).

a) Sexual sins. "The acts of the sinful nature are obvious: sexual immorality, impurity and debauchery" (5:19). *Sexual immorality* includes adultery and fornication. Both are accepted by the world's standards.

Impurity, or uncleanness, refers to a moral impurity. This mind-set delights in the innuendo and the risqué. There is no room for impure thoughts to coexist within the Spirit-filled Christian.

Debauchery, or indecency, denotes an excess or absence of restraint in any area. The Spirit-controlled life practices moderation and balance without dangerous extremes.

b) Religious sin (5:20a). A favorite definition of *idolatry* is from Warren W. Wiersbe's *Be Free:* "Idolatry is simply putting things ahead of God and people. We are to worship God, love people and use things, but too often we use people, love self, and worship things, leaving God out of the picture completely."[3] This definition alerts each of us to the danger of adopting the world's priorities as our own. The golden calf of materialism is an ever-present temptation.

---

[3]Wiersbe, p. 131.

121

In examining the list of works of the flesh, we are apt to slide over *witchcraft* as something that isn't relevant to us today in the twentieth century. However, there is too much in the news today regarding witches, sorcery, satanism, demonology, and astrology to ignore it. In Paul's day it meant using drugs or medicine to appeal to occult powers in an attempt to be freed from them. We should be forewarned not to delve into a realm that we little understand.

c) Sins of relationships. "Hatred, discord, jealousy, fits of rage, selfish ambition, dissensions, factions and envy" (5:20b-21a). *Hatred,* or enmity, is the opposite of *agape* love. Any feeling then that keeps us from seeing our fellow man as valuable and precious is hate. This wouldn't have to be limited to an enraged loathing but could even include dislike, or slight aversion, a "loving-less than." This hatred easily leads to *discord* or strife, quarreling, or fighting with words.

Jealousy is often a source of hatred but also a result of it. Very closely tied to envy, it causes you to want what others have and keeps you from rejoicing at their good fortune.

Fits of rage or outbursts of anger seem to be in direct contradiction to a controlled, balanced, Spirit-filled life. The rage or anger is not simply an inner indignation, but an outward expression of the inner rage.

Ambition in and of itself is not a sin, but *selfish ambition* is. Some are so intent on excelling or "arriving" that they carelessly step on anyone in their path as they climb to the top.

Dissensions, or divisions, and *factions,* or sects, both refer to destroying the unity of a group. It is especially painful to see dissension and factions among God's people who should be united with His unbreakable bond of grace, peace, and love.

Envy, the feeling of displeasure produced by hearing of the prosperity of others, seems harmless enough in our world until we realize it was *envy* that crucified Jesus. "For he [Pilate] knew it was out of envy that they had handed Jesus over to him" (Matthew 27:18). Such a destructive emotion should be feared and fought.

Murder is included in a number of Greek manuscripts and therefore in some translations. Many of us who wouldn't consider murder harbor the anger in our hearts that Jesus equates with murder in Matthew 5:21-22. The murderous thought cannot exist in the Spirit-filled heart.

d) Sins associated with paganism. "Drunkenness, orgies, and the like. I warn you, as I did before, that those who live like this will not inherit the kingdom of God" (5:21b). *Drunkenness* is accepted in today's world and is given a more acceptable name—alcoholism or a hereditary disease. Accepted or not, habitual intoxication keeps a person from being able to control thoughts and actions and causes the individual to make irrational decisions, to come to irresponsible conclusions.

Orgies, or carousing, describes excessive feasting, which included excessive drinking. Any who live like this are not seeking the kingdom and therefore will not inherit the kingdom.

This section ends with a warning that this life-style isn't in harmony with the kingdom of God. The "kingdom of God" can refer to the present rule of God in the Christian's life or a future life in heaven. The present rule of God in the Christian's life involves the will of God. Jesus made them parallel to each other in His prayer in Matthew 6:10. However, it appears that the meaning of "kingdom of God" in 5:21 has a future sense, as it does in other passages. "Do you not know that the wicked will not inherit the *kingdom of God*? Do not be deceived: Neither the sexually immoral nor idolaters nor adulterers nor male prostitutes nor homosexual offenders nor thieves nor the greedy nor drunkards nor slanderers nor swindlers will inherit the *kingdom of God*" (1 Corinthians 6:9-10, emphasis added). "For of this you can be sure: No immoral, impure or greedy person—such a man is an idolater—has any inheritance in the *kingdom of Christ and of God*" (Ephesians 5:5, emphasis added).

3. Fruit of the Spirit (5:22-24). "But the fruit of the Spirit is love, joy, peace, patience, kindness, goodness, faithfulness, gentleness, and self-control. Against such things there is no law." The acts of the sinful nature are contrasted with the fruit of the Spirit even by the categories—acts and fruit. Acts, we commit or perform. Fruit is produced by the Spirit, not by our actions and performance. The fruit of the Spirit will grow and be produced in the lives of Christians when we willingly yield to the Spirit all the works of the flesh. This fruit cannot be genuinely perfected by our human nature.

The first fruit of the Spirit, *love,* seems to be the most important because the others are a result of having this special love in our hearts. This *agape* love is unconditional. It is the kind God had for the world when He gave His Son, the kind God expects us to have for our brothers and sisters in Christ and also for the lost. It is a love that realizes that people are valuable and precious simply because they are part of God's creation. It is a divine love that surpasses any human feeling of affection or family devotion.

When our hearts are filled with *agape* love, we have an inner *joy*, a delight, even in the midst of trials (James 1:1-2) and suffering (Romans 5:3-4), knowing that the hard times will be productive later of maturity and hope.

Love and joy lead to the *peace* that we can experience when we are no longer at war with God. We're at peace with Him because we've yielded ourselves to the Spirit. We no longer try to find room for the human or sinful nature to coexist with the Spirit. We've given up all the anger, bitterness, hatred, envy, and jealousy that keep us from accepting God's divine love that He pours so lavishly into our hearts. This peace surpasses or is even better than understanding (Philippians 4:7).

Patience, or forbearance or long-suffering, is the quality that enables us to endure in the midst of provocation from others. If we really love people, the patience we have with them will be genuine, not just an outward show while we inwardly seethe.

Kindness and *goodness* are so closely related that in the original text *kindness* can be translated *goodness* of heart. Kindness, then, is an inner quality, and goodness is the outward expression of that kindness.

Faithfulness, or trustworthiness, in personal relationships is possible because of the genuine love we have for one another. We need and want to be dependable.

Gentleness, or meekness, is a controlled strength, power in control. Jesus had infinite power but used it with control for the good of mankind and with humility.

Self-control, or temperance, is sometimes understood to mean being in control of oneself. Probably a truer meaning is to have the inner man, or self, controlled by the Spirit. We give up our right of control to the Spirit. The Spirit controls, then, our desires, motives, attitudes, emotions, and feelings, which in turn causes our actions to fall in line accordingly.

Paul ended this section on the fruit of the Spirit by stressing his crucifixion theme (2:20; 6:14): "Those who belong to Christ Jesus have crucified the sinful nature with its passions and desires" (5:24). When you have been crucified with Christ (2:20) and are living as a free man in Christ (5:1, 13), you have made a radical break with sin and are living a life in harmony with that break. "Live as free men, but do not use your freedom as a cover-up for evil; live as servants of God" (1 Peter 2:16). You have received the following freedoms: (1) from sin because Christ died; (2) from guilt because Christ has forgiven you; and (3) from death because Christ has been raised. It is possible for you to misuse your freedoms.

4. Summary (5:25-26). Paul defined living by the Spirit as keeping "in step with the Spirit" (5:25). Paul used Spirit, Spirit of God, and Spirit of Christ interchangeably. "You, however, are controlled not by the sinful nature but by the Spirit, if the Spirit of God lives in you. And if anyone does not have the Spirit of Christ, he does not belong to Christ" (Romans 8:9). Hence, a life in step with the Spirit is one that is in harmony with the Spirit of Christ and the Spirit of God.

Paul warned the Galatians to "not become conceited, provoking and envying each other" (5:26). Being conceited is a departure from being humble. Provoking is a combatant attitude. Envying involves jealousy. Paul's next chapter gives positive direction on the kind of interaction that a Christian under the Spirit's control will have with his brothers and sisters.

Application for Today

Chapter 5 begins the final section of Galatians and embodies the practical implication of chapters 3 and 4—freedom. One of the major objectives of Paul's opponents was to make slaves of his converts. "This matter arose because some false brothers had infiltrated our ranks to spy on the freedom we have in Christ Jesus and to make us slaves" (2:4). "But now that you know God—or rather are known by God—how is it that you are turning back to those weak and miserable principles? Do you wish to be enslaved by them all over again?" (4:9). "Therefore, brothers, we are not children of the slave woman, but of the free woman" (4:31).

Life in Christ was meant to be a joy, not a burden. Slavery has never been the desired life-style of any generation. Being burdened with a yoke would be depressing to anyone. A life that possesses the Spirit of God will show the fruit of joy (5:22). It has been said, "Joy is the flag that is flown from the castle of a man's heart when the king is in residence there."

What freedom does the Christian possess? First, every Christian has been freed from his sins (1:4). When one has been truly freed, he will not fear being thrown back into prison. The Christian has not been paroled; he has been freed!

Second, the Christian has been freed from spiritual death. The law could not give life (3:21) to the dead, but the grace of God can regenerate and give life. Physical life is so precious that man goes to great lengths to sustain it. When a life is sustained or lengthened, much gratitude is expressed. How much more gratitude should Christians express for their life in Jesus, which replaces the sentence of spiritual death that they were under.

In addition to emphasizing freedom, Paul gave a stern warning about falling from grace. It is important to begin the Christian race (5:7), but it is of equal importance to finish the race. What are the reasons that Christians leave the grace of Christ? One of the reasons is found in Galatians—allowing false teachers to cut in. "You were running a good race. Who cut in on you and kept you from obeying the truth?" (5:7). Every Christian must continually examine the Scriptures (Acts 17:11) when anyone teaches or preaches.

Another reason some Christians never finish the race is that they allow the devil to overtake them. "Be self-controlled and alert. Your enemy the devil prowls around like a roaring lion looking for someone to devour" (1 Peter 5:8). Sometimes the devil overtakes unsuspecting Christians through the influence of bad company. "Do not be misled: 'Bad company corrupts good character' " (1 Corinthians 15:33). Every Christian should be careful about relationships that would lead him away from Christ.

Some Christians leave the Lord because they fail to mature. A small boy fell out of bed in the middle of the night, and his father helped him back into bed. The next morning at the breakfast table, his father asked him why he fell out of bed. He said, "I went to sleep too close to where I got in." Some Christians settle down too close to where they begin. "But grow in the grace and knowledge of our Lord and Savior Jesus Christ. To him be glory both now and forever!" (2 Peter 3:18).

Satan attempts to keep people from the Lord on three fronts. First, he seeks to keep them from becoming Christians. He will reason against God and throw other roadblocks in their way. Second, if he fails to keep individuals from becoming Christians, he will try to win them back. Any discouragement he can muster will be used to urge Christians to leave the Lord. However, if these efforts end in failure, he has one final major effort—render Christians useless. Christians who are no threat to the work of Satan do not bother him.

Chapter 5 concludes with the choice of two directions—
acts of the sinful nature or the fruit of the Spirit. The
Christian must take responsibility for the choice he
makes. The end of the choice has eternal consequences—
the kingdom of God (5:21) or the kingdom of Satan.

Thought Questions for Chapter Ten

1. What does it mean to be free in Christ. What are
   we free from?
2. How do people fall away from God?
3. How can we apply "love your neighbor as yourself"
   among Christians?
4. How does one overcome sinful acts?
5. How can you possess the fruit of the Spirit?

CHAPTER
ELEVEN

LIFE OF LIBERTY
—PART II

C. Life of Love (6:1-10)

In 5:26, Paul gave explicit directives on how we are not to treat one another (provoking or envying), and in this section he provided instructions on how we should treat one another.

1. Bearing burdens (6:1-5). Paul began this section with "brothers," his way of introducing a major thought. His primary emphasis in this section is how to deal with a fallen brother.

"Caught" indicates a lack of caution on the part of the fallen. It can be translated as "surprised," "over-taken," or "detected." When the Christian lets his guard down, Satan takes advantage of the opportunity to recapture one of his lost citizens.

The fruit of legalism is best seen in how sin is dealt with. The legalist tends to deal harshly with others because he feels he is right and infallible in his perceptions. Paul was nearly killed in Jerusalem because some legalistic Jews thought he had defiled the temple (Acts 21:27-32). A legalist can condemn without facts because he needs only suspicions or rumors to cause him to act. When a Christian is trapped in sin, he needs restoration, not condemnation.

The way a legalistic Christian and a spiritual person (one who lives by the Spirit, is led by the Spirit, and has the fruit of the Spirit) handle the brother who is caught in sin can be contrasted in three areas. The first area is *aim*. The Christian living by grace seeks to restore while the legalist exploits his brother. *Restore* means "to reset a broken bone." The spiritual brother wants to restore his brother caught in sin because that is painful to the body. The legalist condemns and puts down the fallen in order to make himself look good. He lives by a competitive spirit and compares himself to others (6:4).

A second area is *approach*. The Christian living by grace restores "gently" while the legalist is harsh and insensitive. The spiritual person performs his "gentle restoration" looking carefully at himself. The legalist approaches the fallen with haughty pride because he sees himself as being better than the fallen (see Luke 18:9-14 for the attitude of the self-righteous).

The third area of contrast is *attitude*. The Spirit-led Christian approaches the situation in a spirit of humility and love while the legalist has an attitude of pride and condemnation. The spiritual Christian knows that were it not for the grace of God, he might be the fallen one. He knows that he can be tempted in the same way as the fallen Christian. The word for sin communicates not an isolated act but a settled life-style. The Christian saved by grace realizes that all Christians are vulnerable to isolated acts of sin. The legalist approaches the fallen with a boastful attitude filled with criticism and ostracism. Paul discouraged our comparing ourselves to others: "Each one should test his own actions. Then he can take pride in himself, without comparing himself to somebody else" (6:4).

The legalist adds burdens to others. During the Jerusalem conference, Paul urged his brothers not to put a burden on the new Gentile converts that they themselves might not be able to bear (Acts 15:10). Jesus blasted the legalistic religion because of the heavy loads they expect people to carry: "The teachers of the law and the Pharisees sit in Moses' seat. So you must obey them and do everything they tell you. But do not do what they do, for they do not practice what they preach. They tie up heavy loads and put them on men's shoulders, but they themselves are not willing to lift a finger to move them" (Matthew 23:2-4).

A relationship with God should lighten your burdens and make them bearable. God is depicted as a burden-bearer. "Cast your cares on the LORD and he will sustain you; he will never let the righteous fall" (Psalm 55:22). Even though Jesus denounced the cities of Korazin, Bethsaida, and Capernaum (Matthew 11:20-24), He offered to be a burden-bearer. "Come to me, all you who are weary and burdened, and I will give you rest. Take my yoke upon you and learn from me, for I am gentle and humble in heart, and you will find rest for your souls. For my yoke is easy and my burden is light" (Matthew 11:28-30). When Jesus bears your burdens, your load is lighter.

Paul's emphasis on burden-bearing isn't purely intellectual. He knew from firsthand experience the relief that fellow Christians can supply. For example, he felt that Titus was a burden-bearer. "For when we came into Macedonia, this body of ours had no rest, but we were harassed at every turn—conflicts on the outside, fears within. But God, who comforts the downcast, comforted us by the coming of Titus, and not only by his coming but also by the comfort you had given him" (2 Corinthians 7:5-7).

Galatians 6 teaches that every Christian should help shoulder the burdens that are too heavy for his brother to bear. In helping to shoulder someone else's burdens, you fulfill the law of Christ. "Carry each other's burden, and in this way you will fulfill the law of Christ" (6:2). The law of Christ is best defined as loving one another (Galatians 5:14; see John 13:34; 15:12). However, in nearly the same breath, Paul urged each Christian to bear his own load: "For each one should carry his own load" (6:5). This statement doesn't contradict verse 2 but is a contrast of loads. The "load" of 6:5 is the soldier's pack, an individual responsibility, which is borne by all Christians, but the "burden" of 6:2 is an overwhelming burden that must be shared.

Jesus often found Himself in conflict with the legalists in dealing with fallen and needy people. In John 8:1-11, He confronted the legalists about their treatment of the woman caught in adultery. It was obvious that the woman's accusers weren't interested in her as a person but were only using her as an object of debate with Jesus. They really didn't care about the woman; their intent was to put Jesus in a bad light. In this case, their religion didn't keep them from promoting their selfish interests.

Jesus' love for the fallen is beautifully portrayed in the story found in Luke 7:36-48. The Pharisee's attitude toward the "sinner woman" revealed his heart. Jesus didn't condone her life-style, but He wanted to lift her burden of guilt. Simon's attitude was one of rejection while Jesus' attitude was one of kindness and love. When the threads of this story are woven into the teachings of Galatians 6:1-5, the Christian's attitude and actions are obvious. Restoring the fallen must be done with the love of the Lord.

2. *Sharing blessings (6:6-10).* It is characteristic of Paul to end his letters with a medley of matters that may not be closely tied together and may not be related to ideas expressed in his letters. His Galatian closing can be worked into the general context of the letter.

Because the teacher has helped the student, the student should share with his teacher (6:6). This idea was reflected in Jesus' teaching (Matthew 10:10; Luke 10:7), and Paul also used it in other places (1 Corinthians 9:14; 1 Timothy 5:18). This verse set the stage for Paul's teaching on sowing and reaping.

The sowing and reaping section was introduced with the statement, "Do not be deceived" (6:7a). This common statement (1 Corinthians 6:9; 15:33; James 1:16) means that we should not be misled or that we should "make no mistake." The question of concern in this passage pertains to the meaning of flesh and spirit. In the previous chapter, Paul contrasted the life led by the Spirit (5:16, 18, 25) with the one led by the flesh (5:13, 19). The results of an emphasis on the flesh and on the fruit of the Spirit are obvious. If you choose a life of fleshly orientation, the end result will be destruction; if you choose a life energized by the Spirit, the end result will be eternal life. Paul was trying to get his young converts to see where they would end up if they continued to live lives based on the flesh.

However, there is another way to look at the sowing and reaping section. If verse 6 is connected to verses 7 and 8, Paul could very well have been accusing the Galatians of paying the wrong preachers! They should have been sharing with him, for if they shared with the false teachers, they were sowing in the wrong field. Since the false teachers wanted the Galatians to be zealous for them (4:17), it's possible that the Galatians were paying them.

Verses 7 and 8 contain a universal message that can be divided into three parts. First, you will reap what you sow. In farming, the seed placed in the ground is directly connected with the crop produced. Second, you will reap more than you sow. The farmer expects to reap what he sows, but he also expects to harvest more than he has planted. Hosea wrote of sowing to the wind and reaping a whirlwind—he reaped more than he sowed (Hosea 8:7). Third, you will reap later than you sow. It is not always easy to see the results of your labor as soon as you would like to see it. In fact, the next generation might benefit more from your sowing than you do. In John 4, Jesus had an encounter with the Samaritan woman that resulted in many of the Samaritans believing in Jesus (verse 39). Years later, a traveling evangelist went into that same area and had a great reception to the Word of God (Acts 8:12). Did Jesus' work with the woman and her subsequent "personal evangelism" result in a great harvest in Acts 8? We may not be able to know for sure, but it does supply an interesting connection.

Every decision has a corresponding reward for this life and the one beyond. You invest (sow) either in the flesh or in the Spirit. Life is full of decisions. You must be willing to accept the blessings and the consequences of decisions. The story is told of a young farmer who became angry with his neighbor and sowed Johnson-grass all over his neighbor's farm. Johnsongrass is a dreaded enemy of the farmer because of its harm to crop production. The young farmer received great satisfaction in getting "even" with his neighbor. However, some years passed, and the young farmer fell in love with the other farmer's daughter and eventually married her. When her father died, he inherited the farm and spent the rest of his life trying to rid it of the hated Johnsongrass!

Paul urged his readers not to give up, though they became tired and were tempted to quit. Everyone has at some time fervently taken on a task only to find that as the days go by, the excitement diminishes, and the temptation to quit settles in. Weariness can be found in building projects, pursuing an education, undertaking a physical fitness program, working at a job, and even establishing a Christian marriage. When the going gets tough, the tough get going! Tough times won't last, but tough people will.

Paul admonished the churches of Galatia to do good to all people, but especially to the family of God. No one in God's spiritual family should lack for anything as long as he has spiritual brothers and sisters. Being a part of a forever instant family is a part of God's eternal plan for the church (Ephesians 3:10).

D. Conclusion (6:11-18)

This is Paul's parting "shot" at those who were responsible for his letter—the false teachers. He took one last jab at his opponents and reaffirmed the emphasis of his ministry.

1. Summary of the letter (6:11-13). Paul's normal procedure was to let someone else write the letter as he dictated it, and then he would simply sign his name to it. However, it appears from verse 11 that Paul had written the letter himself. There is a possibility that someone else had been writing the letter and Paul had simply taken the pen in hand and finished it himself.

The "large letters" suggest a number of ideas. Perhaps Paul was going blind and needed to write larger (2 Corinthians 12:7-10; Galatians 4:14-15). However, it is more likely that he was writing in large letters for emphasis. Perhaps inherent in the "large letters" was the idea that "kindergarten" or "baby people" wrote this way, so Paul was writing to babies in "baby language." The preferred idea is that he didn't want them to miss what he was about to say.

The motivation behind the Judaizers' teachings was a desire to be popular—they wanted to "avoid being persecuted for the cross of Christ" (6:12b). They sought the praise of men by making "a good impression" (6:12a). If the Galatians were circumcised, the false teachers could return to Judea and boast about their complete gospel. Such an evangelistic report would put them in good favor with other Jews who didn't understand the implications of the gospel. This kind of evangelism would have appeased even some of their Jewish friends who saw them still practicing and teaching Jewish rites even though they claimed allegiance to Jesus. If one stood for the all-sufficiency of the cross of Christ to save, persecution would come from the Jewish elements because of their denial of a works-righteousness salvation, as well as from the Judaizers who, in spite of their faith in Jesus, still had the same orientation.

Paul's final attack on the Judaizers questioned their sincerity (6:13). He claimed that law-keeping preachers didn't even keep the law; yet they wanted the Galatians to. What was their motivation? Boasting! They were looking for a brag sheet of converts. Paul knew that the Judaizers' method of evangelism wouldn't work on the front or back end (retention) of conversion. Their only method of getting numbers was to follow Paul's work and confuse the new converts. Paul had already accused them of wanting the Galatians to be zealous for them by alienating them from him (4:17). Now he was questioning their motivation.

2. Centrality of the cross (6:14-16). Paul's boasting was in the cross of Christ (6:14a) while the Judaizers boasted of their law-keeping. The cross of Christ represented salvation without human merit as opposed to a salvation of human activity, collectively known as "circumcision," the epitome of human effort. The cross changed Paul's relationship with God and the world. The world, and all that it represented, no longer had a hold on Paul. A world that praised human effort, self-confidence (Philippians 3:3-6), and boasting had lost its appeal to him. His fervent desire was to have a relationship with Christ (Philippians 3:7-11).

In summarizing his letter, Paul put circumcision in its proper place. "Neither circumcision nor uncircumcision means anything; what counts is a new creation" (6:15). The cross that creates the new creation makes the whole subject of circumcision null and void! What appeal did circumcision have in light of the opportunity to become a part of the new creation? This new creation created by the cross is God's real Israel. It isn't unusual for Paul and other writers to refer to the church in Old Testament terminology (Philippians 3:3; James 1:1).

Paul pronounced a blessing on all who follow the standard (rule) that he set forth. The standard of the cross (6:14) and its resulting new creation (6:15) are the sources of peace and mercy. The grace and mercy of God results in peace (1:3).

This conclusion highlighted the differences between Paul and his opponents. Paul hoped that his words would wake up the Galatians and get them back on the right track (5:7). It was breaking his heart to see his work being destroyed.

3. Personal appeal (6:17-18). Until this time most of Paul's arguments against the Judaizers had been polemic and not personal, but this time he was extremely personal. He declared that he had been marked (branded) for the cross of Christ. He had marks that the Judaizers didn't have. The Judaizers might be persuasive in their arguments for a salvation by works, but they hadn't paid the price of following God, as Paul had. Soldiers, slaves, and devotees to pagan religions received marks indicating who or whose they were. Paul saw himself as a soldier in the army of God (Ephesians 6:10-18), slave of Jesus Christ (Romans 1:1), and one who was completely devoted to God (Galatians 2:20).

Paul began his letter with grace (1:3) and ended it with grace: "The grace of our Lord Jesus Christ be with your spirit, brothers" (6:18). He wanted the grace of the Lord Jesus Christ to be with them. In spite of his being upset with them, he still referred to them as "brothers."

It isn't clear what Paul expected to happen when the Galatians received this letter. However, it is clear that he did write the letter out of deep concern for them and desired the best for them. Subsequent history doesn't support the idea that these churches in south Galatia ever ridded themselves of the yoke of slavery they had embraced. History doesn't support the idea of strong churches in Antioch of Pisidia, Lystra, Derbe, or Iconium. Paul's prediction that accepting the new gospel would result in their falling away (5:4) apparently came to pass. If this fact is true, Paul lived the rest of his life knowing that an important part of his life's work had been undone. He knew it wouldn't affect his salvation (1 Corinthians 3:12-15), but the pain was still there. Perhaps this experience led him to write a letter to his sweetheart church (Philippians) and warn them of similar teachers coming to them

(Philippians 3:1-3). He never wanted to write a "Galatian letter" again.

Galatians is a bulwark for all generations and civilizations as to the meaning of the cross. It needs to be restudied in every generation to make sure that a "different gospel" hasn't been accepted. Man tends to become legalistic and to see "essentials" to salvation that Paul didn't see. There is a tendency to "add to" the work of God. There is a little legalism in all of us, so it behooves the best of us to reexamine *our* gospel in light of *the* gospel and to make sure that we aren't running our race in vain (2:2).

A life motivated by inner desire instead of outer demand is exemplary of God's new creation and is full of joy. God's great scheme for us includes our seeing the importance of the spirit and attitude behind our actions as opposed to seeing only the end result of our actions. Suppose I decide some Saturday morning at breakfast to vacuum the living room and clean off the dining room table while my wife is at the store. I am glowing inside with the excitement of such a surprise. I anxiously await my wife's leaving so I can perform my surprise. As my wife leaves the house, she turns and says, "Would you vacuum the living room and clean off the dining room table while I'm gone?" I do it, but not with the same attitude. The results are the same, but my conduct during the performance is not.

The Galatian letter is not an intellectual polemic against law-keeping systems that promise the favor of God, but it is a declaration of the type of inner drive God desires for all His children. Being in every respect (outward and inward) what God desires us to be is the product of the grace of God. When all is said and done, the epithet of every Christian will read: "Here lies a sinner saved by the grace of God."

Application for Today

Chapter 6 is the last section of Paul's application of the gospel of grace. This chapter begins with a challenge to be involved in the lives of others: "Brothers, if someone is caught in a sin, you who are spiritual should restore him gently. But watch yourself, or you also may be tempted. Carry each other's burdens, and in this way you will fulfill the law of Christ" (6:1-2).

It is clear from the Scriptures that every Christian should be interested in "restoring" and "carrying." These are functions that the body does for the benefit and preservation of itself. Ask yourself the following questions:

1. When was the last time I sought to restore a fallen family member?
2. Do I feel any responsibility to go and correct those in sin, or do I believe only the elders or preachers should do it?
3. What burdens have I carried for others?

These questions challenge us to apply the gospel of grace in everyday life. Christianity is a manner of life, not just a theory. Sunday "talk" needs to be translated into the Monday "walk."

Christians must help those in need without concern for repayment. There will come a time in the lives of all Christians when help will be needed, whether it be physical or spiritual. Realizing how much God has given and forgiven us should be the spark to ignite us to help others.

This chapter contains one of the great principles of life. "Do not be deceived: God cannot be mocked. A man reaps what he sows. The one who sows to please his sinful nature, from that nature will reap destruction; the one who sows to please the Spirit, from the Spirit will reap eternal life" (6:7-8). This great principle can be applied to many areas of life. Everyone who has ever chosen to participate in illicit sex or alcohol or drug use can testify as to the consequences he will reap. On the other hand, those who invest their lives in helping and assisting others will reap benefits beyond any physical repayment. To give and meet the needs of others can be demanding and exhausting; hence, Paul encouraged his readers not to quit. "Let us not become weary in doing good, for at the proper time we will reap a harvest if we do not give up" (6:9).

The Christian's concern should not be limited to other Christians but should include a larger group. "Therefore, as we have opportunity, let us do good to all people" (6:10). What is the average local congregation known for in its community? Is it referred to as the group that does not use an instrument in worship or whose preacher isn't called "reverend"? Wouldn't it be great for the church to be known as a friend to the homeless and needy? Jesus spoke of the Christian's need to influence the world so that God might be praised: "In the same way, let your light shine before men, that they may see your good deeds and praise your Father in heaven" (Matthew 5:16).

The world is looking for a church that translates Christianity into a living reality. The church should be seen more as an organism than as an organization with well-oiled machinery. Our buildings should never replace the movement of Jesus. The book of Galatians assists the Christian in translating the doctrine of Christ into a way of life.

From Slavery to Sonship

Thought Questions for Chapter Eleven

1. What should be the attitude and actions of Christians toward fallen Christians?
2. How should you go about restoring someone who has left the Lord?
3. Give some examples (positive and negative) of sowing and reaping.
4. How does the teaching of Luke 10:30-37 relate to Galatians 6:10?
5. Give examples of overwhelming burdens that you have experienced. How were the burdens shared? Give examples of individual responsibilities that should not be shared.

CHAPTER TWELVE

LEGALISM: THE DESTROYER OF LIFE WITH GOD

Purpose of Galatians

The book of Galatians provides one side of the most significant debate of the early church—how mission work should be conducted among non-law-keeping Gentiles. The gospel had found success among the children of Abraham (Acts 13:26) and the Gentiles who worshiped God (Acts 13:16) and who were also known as God-fearers (Acts 13:26). Paul's first missionary journey was the impetus for forming churches composed of disciples who didn't have a background of monotheism (Acts 14:11-13). The people in most pagan cultures didn't have the ethical behavior that characterized the Jews and other God-fearing people. Paul's method for evangelizing these pagan cultures was to preach that the gospel of grace was sufficient to save. Christ, who was now formed within the new disciples (2:20; 4:19), became the foundation for their ethical behavior.

Because Paul had been throughout the Galatian area preaching and appointing leaders (Acts 14:23), he felt that he was leaving the disciples on the path leading to Christian growth and transformation. However, without his knowledge, a group of false brothers (2:4)

144

arrived, preaching a different gospel from the one he had preached. Those Jewish brothers were simply trying to be sure that the new Christians were like them, so they weren't even aware that they were false teachers. Their evangelistic method consisted of preaching the same facts about Jesus that Paul had preached, and they also agreed with Paul's teaching on faith and baptism (3:26-27). However, they felt additional works were necessary for salvation (Acts 15:1). Since these works were considered to be redemptive, the false brothers implied that the gospel of grace was insufficient. The clash between Paul and the false brothers was rooted in the essence of the gospel. Paul preached salvation by grace (plus nothing), and his opponents preached salvation by grace plus law (circumcision and ceremony).

The conflict between Paul and the false teachers wasn't in the facts of the gospel but in the implication of those facts. Even though there were similarities in the "two gospels," the differences were extremely serious (1:6-9). Paul's opponents' motivation was good. They never intended for the new Christians to keep the whole law (5:3), but just enough of the law so the new believers could have the same orientation as they did. The emphasis on law provided a checklist for the "older brothers" to decide if the new brothers were really orthodox in all their Christianity.

Nature of Legalism

Legalism involves setting standards not revealed in the gospel that are considered to have inherent redemptive merit. There is nothing wrong with setting standards unless those standards are worshiped and placed on a par with the gospel. Legalism is marked by confidence in personal performance as opposed to confidence in the work of God at the cross.

Legalism is a foe of the sufficiency of the gospel of grace. For one to maintain that an activity after salvation has merit toward salvation is to proclaim the inefficiency of an infinite God to save without human effort. To deny meritorious acts beyond salvation doesn't imply that salvation by grace waives a life of dedicated response, however. The recipient of the greatest blessing ever given will express gratitude until his day of graduation into the eternal presence of the One who redeemed him.

Legalism creates a wrong focus. Since legalism sees changed or controlled behavior as true evidence of Christianity, the quickest means of achieving behavior changes becomes very important. The shortcut to these changes involves outer restraints rather than an inner restraint. An outer restraint is effective, provided the consequence is greater than the effort, the rewards are fulfilling, and adequate pressure exists. Outer restraint works if the circumstances are conducive. A true inner restraint promotes stimuli for change and proper conduct regardless of consequences, rewards, pressure, or circumstances. An inner restraint finds it dynamic in who you really are rather than in how you portray yourself to be. An inner restraint comes from a relationship with the Creator.

Legalism considers Christian activities as premium payments on the purchase of salvation rather than thank-you notes for the gift of salvation. Christian activity from the viewpoint of either "premium payments" or "thank-you notes" looks basically the same, but the heart of the believer doing either one won't be the same. When you write a monthly check for your car payment, you don't write it with the same joy and enthusiasm as you would if it were a thank-you note for the privilege of free driving! A gift generates more love and appreciation than "pay as you go" ever will. A gift creates a loving, generous response.

Danger of Legalism

Legalism is dangerous when it consistently requires too much human effort; it will cause only discouragement and frustration. Having high Christian expectations is good; however, when these expectations are viewed as being redemptive, either consciously or unconsciously, no provision is made for the days when the expectations aren't met. It isn't hard for a hitter to stay high when he is getting a hit every time he is at bat, but when he has a long series of strikeouts, he knows his job is in jeopardy because of poor performance. Legalism doesn't provide for bad days (or weeks or months), and failure to meet high expectations creates frustration and despair. The way to spell relief from the merry-go-round of frustration and despair is Q-U-I-T! The bank of human merit has experienced an overdraft so high it can never be repaid. Personal bankruptcy is filed with a resolve never to purchase again on the payment plan. When you stop beating your head against the wall, it feels so good that you promise never to do it again.

Legalism that requires little response is dangerous on the other extreme. A shallow redemptive response that is easily met creates a sense of satisfaction and complacency resulting in stagnation. When you can easily achieve the low-expectation level, you have no desire to learn more or to respond differently since the premium payments are being met with some to spare.

Legalism is dangerous because its orientation (law) for Christian living is wrong. Legalism attempts to enforce Christian guidelines from the perspective of law rather than from the perspective of Jesus. Christianity does have guidelines, but when you depend on the dynamic of law rather than on Jesus, you invite trouble. Christian behavior derived from law will do well for a while and many visible changes will occur quickly, but that which was to give life will be the destroyer of life. When Paul was teaching the Galatians, his "method" for changed and sustained growth was "Christ in you" (Galatians 4:19; see Colossians 1:27). When the young Galatian converts accepted a different gospel, Paul didn't scrap his method but repeated it: "My dear children, for whom I am again in the pains of childbirth until Christ is formed in you" (4:19). His approach to Christian behavior and growth was right the first time, so he wasn't about to change because it took a "second dose."

Legalism that requires too much or too little will destroy life. Legalism demanding too much will push a person through the cracks and back into the world. The "low-grade" legalism allows a person to stay on the church roll when his heart is in the world. He will no longer be "taking church" for credit but will only be auditing the course!

A doctrinal legalism that requires adherence to truth on ten thousand different issues destroys any hope for world evangelism. This type of legalism keeps leaders busy keeping their own people convinced and reindoctrinated on the issues and leaves little time to really confront the world with their "gospel." Their confrontation is basically hopeless since they can't keep their "own" in line much less convince the average unbeliever of all the ten thousand points of doctrine.

The alternative to all legalism is the gospel of grace, which saves and enables the Christian to sustain this newfound relationship with God. The gospel of grace will result in a greater response with a more willing attitude than law could ever achieve. Paul, the Hebrew of Hebrews, is living testimony to the truth of this proposition.

Grace and Legalism Contrasted

The young Christians in Galatia weren't prepared to recognize the Judaizers' false gospel. The Pharisees had an abundance of religious words and phrases that could lull a young Christian into accepting "their" gospel without question. Using biblical terms and being able to quote verses aren't always proof of rightness. The motives behind legalism are good (to be acceptable to God and to be more spiritual), but the danger comes when legalism becomes an end in itself rather than a means to the end. Methods tend to puff you up and make you believe you are superspiritual while others are inferior. Legalism is worshiping the standards that were designed to make you more spiritual.

Extremes must be avoided when studying grace and law. However, two possible extremes would be law without grace or grace without law. Paul didn't have a total disdain for the law because he saw it as "holy, righteous and good" (Romans 7:12). But the law was not a remedy for man's sinful condition. Grace has always been the means for saving men; for example, David was saved by grace under law but not by law.

Legalism is natural to human experience since the world stresses human effort and competition. Legalism seems safer than grace because it has definite guidelines. Insecure people feel life is out of control unless they have prescribed limits and rules. A religion of rules and regulations is easier to teach than it is to show one how to develop a relationship with God.

One of the major contrasts between legalism and grace is despair and peace. A legalistic system creates despair because you can't consistently keep its standards. The struggle in Romans 7:17-25 shows the burden you bear when you attempt to save yourself with law. However, about the time the law-keeping legalist feels good about his law-keeping, someone ups the law expectations, and he is hopelessly behind again.

When you live under grace, you experience the peace of God (Philippians 4:6-8). You are what you are by the grace of God (1 Corinthians 15:10). You know that you are loved and accepted, no matter where you are on the road to God, whereas the legalist has a standard of acceptance. When the legalist lives above his standard, he prides himself on his religion (Luke 18:9-14). When he lives below his standard, he is in spiritual depression.

Grace and legalism can also be contrasted in their view of salvation. In legalism, salvation depends on keeping God's every command. Under grace, salvation depends on a submissive spirit that strives to please God in all areas of life. Legalism tends to create feelings of insecurity and adds doubt as to one's worth in the sight of God. The legalist can never really be sure that he knows enough of the law to be saved or that his obedience to what he does know is adequate for a right standing with God.

The true disciple of Jesus is definitely interested in keeping His commands. However, his command-keeping isn't a result of complying with a written code that carries consequences if it is violated—it is a response to Jesus! Keeping commandments is a fruit of surrender to one who has joyfully accepted Him.

Sometimes preaching grace makes us nervous because we see it as being synonymous with salvation by faith only (without baptism). To allay that nervousness, we feel that something always needs to be said about obedience. Yet, we wouldn't be upset if we heard a sermon on obedience that didn't mention grace. It is important to study salvation by grace and to feel comfortable with what the Bible teaches.

There is danger in reacting to any extreme. Paul headed off a reaction to legalism by stating that grace can't be a license to act however you please (5:13-15). One example of reacting to grace is seen in some preachers' sermons—they only warn that you can fall from it! Some religious groups teach the importance of grace in salvation but live as if they are saved by good deeds. On the other hand, some who emphasize works or deeds as important to a relationship with God live as if they were saved by grace and nothing else!*

Thought Questions for Chapter Twelve

1. What is the difference between being legalistic and abiding by the Scriptures?
2. What is the difference in the approach to the Scriptures by a legalist as opposed to a liberal?
3. How has legalism or liberalism hurt the church?
4. Can any of God's commands be perverted into legalism?
5. How can the Christian stay balanced in his relationship with God and other Christians?

---

*This material was published in *Image,* September 1988.

CHAPTER
THIRTEEN

"I HAVE BEEN
CRUCIFIED
WITH CHRIST"

There are at least three reasons why Paul was upset when he wrote the book of Galatians. First, he was under heavy attack from false brethren (2:4). Their assault centered on his credibility and his preaching. Second, because the Galatians had accepted this "different gospel" (1:6), Paul could see his work being destroyed. Third, the essence of the gospel was being challenged. The opponents preached salvation by law-keeping, and Paul preached salvation by grace. If the Galatians accepted the opponents' view, the essential element that makes the gospel truly good news would be demolished.

After Paul expressed his dismay with the Galatian Christians, he established his credibility as a competent teacher, using three major arguments. His first argument pertained to his conversion (1:11-22). His spiritual turnaround could be attributed only to the Lord. His training was directly from God and wasn't the result of secondhand information from other church leaders. Paul's second argument centered on his being approved by the leaders of the church. Barnabas, Titus, and Paul visited with the Jerusalem leaders and discussed the missionary efforts among the Gentile nations. The leaders' conclusion was that Paul's message was complete (2:6), and they gave him "the right hand of fellowship" (2:9). Paul's third argument was a demonstration (2:11-21). The heart of this argument was his rebuke of Peter's hypocrisy (2:13). This rebuke gave Paul true credibility in the eyes of all.

The conclusion of this first major section of the book revealed the dynamic and drive for Paul's life—Jesus Christ. "I have been crucified with Christ and I no longer live, but Christ lives in me" (2:20). Jesus was responsible for the changes in Paul's life. His life was never the same after he had shared in the crucifixion of Jesus. His earlier days had been characterized by law, but now his life was characterized by faith in the Son of God!

When you are united with Christ in His death, there are changes in your life. If you form an acrostic from the word *crucify*, each letter can represent a result that comes from a relationship with Christ.

Commitment to Serve

Serving should be natural for the disciple of Jesus. Paul gave three ways to demonstrate this service. Preaching the Word is one means of service (1:23). It isn't always well received, but it still must be done. Paul was Exhibit A of the power of his message.

A second way to serve is by telling the truth to fellow Christians (4:16). Sharing truth must be preceded by a relationship (4:12-15). It is obvious that Paul had sacrificed for the Galatians, and they, in turn, were willing to do anything for him. Paul's purpose in telling the truth was to have Christ formed in all believers (4:19).

A third way to serve is by doing good for others (6:9). There's no better feeling to be found than helping someone who needs you. It is true that the giver is more blessed than the receiver (Acts 20:35). A friend of mine is serving time in prison. He claims he is innocent of the crime that sentenced him to seven years. Whether he's guilty or innocent is of little consequence to me; he is a brother in need of encouragement. There's little I can do for him. I haven't been able to visit him since the prison is far from where I live and in an area where I don't travel. However, he can receive mail. I can serve him by sending him an occasional card or letter. It's a comfort for him to know his friends haven't forgotten him.

There are other ways to serve, but Galatians gives these three ways as good examples to imitate. Jesus came to serve (Matthew 20:28), and His twentieth-century followers should imitate His manner of life.

Responding Love

Paul's faith was rooted in the Son of God who loved him to such a degree that He willingly gave Himself. Because of Jesus' great love for him, Paul couldn't help but respond in love. There are three demonstrations of this responsive love in Galatians. The first one is Paul's willingness to suffer pain for the benefit of others (4:19). Because the Galatians had adopted a "different gospel," their first spiritual birth had been aborted. Paul was willing to go through the pains of childbirth a second time for their benefit. His phrase, "my dear children," is evidence of his great love and concern for them.

A second demonstration of responsive love is an active faith (5:6). Expression is the very nature of true faith. Love for God and man is the essence of faith. James spoke to the nature of faith: "But someone will say, 'You have faith; I have deeds.' Show me your faith without deeds, and I will show you my faith by what I do" (James 2:18). Our actions should be based on true love and shouldn't be the result of guilt or duty (1 Corinthians 13:1-3). A parent disciplines his child because he loves him, not because it's enjoyable.

A third demonstration of responsive love is restoring the fallen or wayward (6:1-2). It should be natural for the Christian to want to bring back ones who have strayed away because this attitude is reflective of God (Luke 15). Love compels the Christian to go to the spiritual aid of family members. This demonstration stems from following the "Golden Rule" (Matthew 7:12)—you treat others the way you want to be treated. The law of Christ (6:1-2) demands that you love your neighbor as you love yourself (5:14).

A responsive love shows the overwhelming gratitude for the benefits that you have as a result of your relationship with Christ. There can be no greater love than the love that motivates you to do for others. "Greater love has no one than this, that one lay down his life for his friends" (John 15:13).

Undying Praise

A natural response to God's blessings is praise. David implored God to forgive him of his transgressions and declared how he would respond to this blessed forgiveness.

Save me from bloodguilt, O God,
  the God who saves me,
  and my tongue will sing of your righteousness.
O Lord, open my lips,
  and my mouth will declare your praise (Psalm 51:14-15).

The redeemed one who has participated in the death of Christ lives a life of praise and adoration. Why should you praise God? You should praise Him because of the grace that He bestows (1:3). You have grace because of your position "in Christ," and peace is a result of grace. If you don't believe you are saved by grace, you will never have any real peace.

You should praise God for your redemption (3:14). Your purchase price was expensive. Those who attempted salvation by law were under a curse (3:10), and Jesus became a curse for you so you might be redeemed (3:13). God did for you what you could never have done yourself! Praise God! God always abundantly responds to your needs. "Now to him who is able to do immeasurably more than all we ask or imagine, according to his power that is at work within us" (Ephesians 3:20).

You should praise God for the direction of your life. Paul knew there was some reason for his being saved from a life of Judaism. God clarified His purpose for Paul in Acts 9:15. Paul knew that God was leading him in his mission work with the Gentiles. "For God, who was at work in the ministry of Peter as an apostle to the Jews, was also at work in my ministry as an apostle to the Gentiles" (2:8). It would be nice if God's specific purpose for each Christian was as clear today. However, we do know that all Christians are to live a God-glorifying life. How each of us fulfills that purpose is decided by time and prayer.

You should praise God for life (2:20). This life isn't simply the physical existence; it's a quality of life known only to those who have put their faith and trust in Jesus. Jesus taught He was life and the giver of life: "I am the way and the truth and the life. No one comes to the Father except through me" (John 14:6); "The thief comes only to steal and kill and destroy; I have come that they may have life, and have it to the full" (John 10:10).

You should praise God for your sonship (3:26; 4:6). Prior to becoming Christians, the Gentile readers were slaves to the "basic principles of the world" (4:3, 8) and the Jewish readers were slaves to the law (4:31), but now each of them had an opportunity to be a part of God's family as a son with full rights (4:5). Being a son had more appeal than being a slave. Slaves weren't treated well. They didn't have any benefits or receive any rewards such as "Slave of the Year." Along with sonship went the opportunity to be an heir of the promise to Abraham (3:29).

You can't praise God enough for all you have in Jesus. You can't repay the debt you owe for all the good things you have received—and the best news of all is that you don't have to repay! The song tells us we owed a debt we could not pay, and He paid a debt He did not owe. Surely, such a magnificent God deserves your forever, undying praise!

Cleansing of Sin

All men seek cleansing from their sins. The gospel is "good news" about sin—it can be forgiven! There are three steps necessary for cleansings to take place. The first step on the road to being cleansed was the giving of Christ Himself (1:4). Jesus not only gave Himself, but in giving, He redeemed you from your sins (3:13). Redemption communicates the idea of being purchased from a life of slavery to be a son of God and to be made free.

The second step in cleansing is the rescue mission that Jesus performed (1:4). From a human viewpoint, it looked like "mission impossible," but it was orchestrated by the God of the impossible. Your rescue was in accordance with God's will but not against your will.

The third step in your cleansing took place when you were clothed with Christ (3:27). In Roman culture, a special ceremony was conducted when a boy officially became a man. During the ceremony (usually during the teen years), his toys were burned (see 1 Corinthians 13:11), and a toga was placed on his shoulders. This new clothing "signified" his transformation from boyhood to manhood. Paul used this familiar imagery to communicate a new relationship with God through Christ. Because Christ is your righteousness (1 Corinthians 1:30-31), you are now clothed in a righteousness from God (Philippians 3:9).

Infinite Gratitude

Paul never forgot what God had done for him, and he lived a life of corresponding gratitude (1 Timothy 1:12-17). What answers would Paul give to the question: What are you the most grateful for? One answer would be justification. Galatians 2:15-16 is the heart of the book. In this "heart passage," the word *justify* is obvious. Your justification is based not on your work but on the work of Christ. In these verses Paul mentioned "faith in Christ" as a key to justification. When you understand that *justification* means "to render guiltless," you are grateful for God's work.

Another answer that Paul would give for being grateful is the freedom from unbearable burdens. He admonished the young disciples who had been freed from an unbearable burden to avoid becoming involved with another yoke of slavery (5:1-2). Salvation that stems from human meritorious acts places a burden on you that is impossible to bear. Peter spoke to the validity of this truth: "Now then, why do you try to test God by putting on the necks of the disciples a yoke that neither we nor our fathers have been able to bear?" (Acts 15:10).

Another reason for expressing gratitude has to do with being a new creation. "Neither circumcision nor uncircumcision means anything; what counts is a new creation" (6:15). Paul discounted the importance of circumcision when compared to being a part of a new creation. Man always longs to have new things or new beginnings. The Galatians had once lived a sin-filled life rooted in paganism, but through Jesus, they were given the opportunity to become new.

You should react with overwhelming gratitude for your justification, your freedom from the unbearable, and your gift of being a new creation. Every day you should praise God. The reaction to Paul's preaching was praise for God (1:24).

Forward Look

Becoming a Christian gave Paul a new outlook and lease on life. He had an expectation for the future that was made possible only by his conversion to Christ. Paul looked forward to continued help from God. Salvation isn't a result of human effort, and it isn't sustained by human effort. In one of Paul's arguments on salvation by grace, he asked a series of questions related to the Galatians' experience. One of those questions was this: "After beginning with the Spirit, are you now trying to attain your goal by human effort?" (3:3). The difference between the covenant of Moses and the new covenant is the difference between saying "thou shalt not" and "I will" (Hebrews 8:7-12).

One covenant rests on the ability of man and the other on the character and work of God.

Paul looked forward to being an heir forever. The one who has been clothed in Christ not only belongs to Abraham but also inherits the promise (3:26-29). Paul described Christians as being "heirs of God and co-heirs with Christ"; co-heirs with Christ will share in His glory, provided they also share in His sufferings (Romans 8:17).

Paul looked forward to a future righteousness. "But by faith we eagerly await through the Spirit the righteousness for which we hope" (5:5). Paul viewed righteousness as a present possession and a future state. Righteousness is a result of the Spirit of God.

An anticipation of the future has carried Christians through difficult times. The excitement of going over a hill and seeing a new valley below supplied adrenaline to new settlers. The Christian has the benefit of blessings now with the expectation of more in the future.

Yielding Spirit

With his Pharisee background, Paul grew up in a works-righteousness atmosphere. He considered himself beyond his peers (1:14) and as one who had been superior in law-keeping (Philippians 3:6). He lacked humility while he lived as a law-keeping Pharisee. After his conversion, though, Paul was transformed with a servant heart and a humble spirit.

There are three characteristics of one who has a yielding spirit. First is openness for input. Paul willingly sought the Jerusalem leaders' advice on the message he had been preaching to see if they could suggest changes (2:2). Only a very secure, open person can take the initiative to test his preaching.

Another characteristic of a yielding spirit is a life that is lived in harmony with the Spirit. "Since we live by the Spirit, let us keep in step with the Spirit" (5:25). Living a life in harmony with the Spirit is characterized by Christlikeness and Godlikeness. Paul saw the Spirit, Spirit of God, and Spirit of Christ as being interchangeable. "You, however, are controlled not by the sinful nature but by the *Spirit*, if the *Spirit of God* lives in you. And if anyone does not have the *Spirit of Christ*, he does not belong to Christ" (Romans 8:9, emphasis added).

A third characteristic of a yielding spirit is being a gentle restorer. "Brothers, if someone is caught in a sin, you who are spiritual should restore him gently" (6:1). When you try to help the fallen brother, you should do it with gentleness, care, and concern. The gentle restorer realizes that someday he could be on the other end of the restoration, so he also watches himself.

Conclusion

Galatians 2:20 has unlocked many doors that are pertinent for Christian living. Crucifixion is a theme that can be traced throughout the book of Galatians. In addition to the crucifixion of self (2:20), Paul mentioned crucifying the sinful nature and the world: "Those who belong to Christ Jesus have crucified the sinful nature with its passions and desires" (5:24); "May I never boast except in the cross of our Lord Jesus Christ, through which the world has been crucified to me, and I to the world" (6:14). Jesus calls all men to deny self and to follow Him. Galatians shows the type of following that God expects.

Thought Questions for Chapter Thirteen

1. How does Paul use the word *crucify* in Galatians? (See 2:20; 5:24; 6:14.)
2. What are the five most appreciated blessings from God for which He should be praised?
3. How did you feel when you were cleansed from sin? Have you sustained that feeling? If you have not sustained it, why haven't you? How can you regain it?
4. How can Christians have a positive outlook for their future with so many problems on every side?
5. What keeps Christians from yielding to the will of God?

BIBLIOGRAPHY

Books

Arichea, Daniel C., and Nida, Eugene A. *A Translators Handbook on Paul's Letter to the Galatians.* London: United Bible Societies, 1976.

Bell, R. C. *Studies in Galatians.* Austin, Tex.: Firm Foundation, 1954.

Bruce, F. F. *The Epistle to the Galatians.* Grand Rapids: Zondervan, 1970.

Burton, Ernest DeWitt. *The International Critical Commentary on Galatians.* Edinburgh: T&T Clark, 1921.

Cole, R. A. *Galatians.* Grand Rapids: Eerdmans, 1980.

Guthrie, Donald. *Galatians.* Grand Rapids: Eerdmans, 1981.

Johnson, Robert L. *The Letter of Paul to the Galatians.* Austin, Tex.: R. B. Sweet, 1969.

Ketcherside, W. Carl. *A Study of the Covenants.* Cassville, Mo.: Litho Printers.

Lightfoot, Joseph B. *The Epistle of St. Paul to the Galatians.* Grand Rapids: Zondervan, 1967.

MacArthur, John F. *Liberated for Life.* Glendale: Gospel Light Publications, 1971.

Massey, Jim. *How Galatians Means Me.* Florence, Ala.: International Bible College.

Redderbos, Herman N. *The Epistle of Paul to the Churches of Galatia.* Grand Rapids: Eerdmans, 1965.

Stott, John R. W. *Only One Way the Message of Galatians.* London: Inter-Varsity Press, 1968.

Tenney, Merrill C. *Galatians: The Charter of Christian Liberty.* Grand Rapids: Eerdmans, 1957.

Vaughan, Curtis. *Galatians.* Grand Rapids: Zondervan, 1972.

Vos, Howard F. *Galatians: A Call to Christian Liberty.* Chicago: Moody Press, 1971.

Wharton, Ed. *The Constitution of Christian Freedom.* Lubbock, Tex.: Sunset School of Preaching.

Tapes

Anderson, Lynn. *Letter of Liberty: A Fresh Look at Galatians.* Living Resources, Abilene, Texas.

Atchley, Rich. *The Place of Grace.* 45th Annual Pepperdine University Bible Lectureship, April 19–22, 1988.

Cope, Mike. *The Amazing Power.* Mid-American Evangelism Workshop, Indianapolis, Indiana.

James, Larry. *Believers, Be Free!* Richardson East Church of Christ, Richardson, Texas.

Meador, Prentice. *Galatian Series.* South National Church of Christ, Springfield, Missouri.

Owens, Glenn. *Galatians: Gospel of Grace.* Living Resources, Abilene, Texas.

Articles

Hach, Robert. "Mixing Law and Grace." Mt. View: Boulder, March 16, 1987.

Heitman, Dave. "Sonship vs. Slavery." Mt. View: Boulder, December 21, 1987.

APPENDIX

A Chronology of the Life of Paul

DATE	EVENT	ACTS	LETTERS
5 B.C.–A.D. 30	**Life of Jesus**		
c. Jan. 5 B.C.	Birth of Jesus		
c. 27–30 B.C.	Ministry of Jesus		
April 9, A.D. 30	Resurrection of Jesus		
c. May 18, A.D. 30	Ascension of Jesus	1:3-9	
30–43	**The Church in Palestine**	1:1–11:18	
May 28, 30	Pentecost Sermon of Peter	2:1ff.	
c. 33–34	Persecution over Stephen; scattering to		
	Judea & Samaria	8:1-3	
34	Conversion of Paul	9:1-19	G 1:13; etc.
34–37	Paul in Damascus & Arabia	9:19-23	G 1:15-16
Mar. 37	Death of Tiberius; change of frontier policy		G 1:17-18
	by Caligula		
Late 37	Paul's escape from Damascus (Aretus IV	9:23-25	1 C 11:32-33
	dies [38–40])		

DATE	EVENT	ACTS	LETTERS
Late 37	Paul's First Jerusalem Visit (3-year visit)	9:26-30	G 1:18-19
37–43	Paul in Syria & Cilicia	9:30	G 1:21
	Peter in Palestine (Cornelius)	9:31–11:18	
c. 40	Paul's vision of Paradise		2 C 12:2-4
c. 43	Spread of persecuted as far as Phoenicia, Cyprus, & Antioch; Greeks converted	11:19-21	
43–47	**Paul in Antioch**	11:26–13:3	
c. 43	Barnabas brings Paul to Antioch	11:25-26	
c. 44	Paul in Antioch church for a whole year; prophets come & foretell a famine	11:26-28	
Passover, 44	James killed; Peter imprisoned	12:1-19	
Late 44–Early 45	Herold Agrippa I dies	12:20-23	
c. 46	Famine	11:28	
Early 47	Paul's Second Jerusalem Visit (14-year visit)		G 2:1-10
Early–Mid 47	Disciples at Antioch decide to send aid to Judea in response to apostles' request	11:29	G 2:10
	Paul's Third Jerusalem Visit, (famine visit)	11:30; 12:25	(cf. G 2:10)
	Paul confronts Peter at Antioch		G 2:11 ff.

DATE	EVENT	ACTS	LETTERS
Mid 47–Mid 48	**First Missionary Journey**		
Summer–Fall 47	Paul in Cyprus	13:3–14:26	
Fall 47–Mid 48	Paul in Galatia & Pamphylia	13:4–13	
		13:13–14:26	
Mid 48–Mid 49	**Paul in Antioch**	14:26–15:40	
Mid–Late 48	Paul writes Galatians		
Late 48–Early 49	Judaizers come to Antioch	15:1-2	
Early 49	Paul's Fourth Jerusalem Visit	15:2-30	
	(conference visit)		
Summer 49–Summer 51	**Second Missionary Journey**		
Summer 49	Paul in Syria, Cilicia, Galatia, & Phyrgia	15:41–18:22	
Fall 49	Paul in Macedonia & Athens	15:41–16:6	
	Paul, Silas, & Timothy leave Thessalonica	16:6–18:1	
	& go to Beroea		
	Paul to Athens; leaves Silas & Timothy	17:10	
	behind		
	Paul sends back word for Silas & Timothy	17:14	
	to come as soon as possible		
	Timothy (& Silas?) joins Paul at Athens	17:15	
	Paul stays in Athens, sends Timothy back		1 Th 3:1-2
	to Thessalonica		

167

DATE	EVENT	ACTS	LETTERS
49	Expulsion of Jews from Rome; Priscilla & Aquila to Corinth	18:2	
Dec. 49–June 51	Paul to Corinth; stays 18 mos.	18:1, 11	
c. Jan. 50	Timothy (& Silas?) joins Paul at Corinth	18:5	
c. Jan. 50	Paul, Silas, & Timothy write 1 Thessalonians		1 Th 1:1
Early 50	Paul, Silas, & Timothy write 2 Thessalonians		2 Th 1:1
May 51	Gallio arrives in Corinth	18:12	
June 51	Paul leaves Corinth	18:18	
July 51	Paul's Fifth Jerusalem Visit	18:22	
Aug. 51–May 54	**Third Missionary Journey**		
Aug.–Sept. 51	Paul travels through Galatia, Phrygia, & the upper country	18:23–21:8	
Oct.–Dec. 51	Paul in synagogue in Ephesus	18:23; 19:1	
Jan. 52–July 53	Paul in hall of Tyrannus	19:8	
c. Dec. 52–Jan. 53	Paul writes the previous letter to Corinth concerning the immoral & the contribution	19:9-10	1 C 5:9; 2 C 8:10; 9:1-2
	The Corinthians write to Paul		1 C 7:1
c. Jan.–Mar. 53	Paul sends Timothy & Erastus into Macedonia	19:22	
c. Mar. 53	Paul plans for Timothy to visit Corinth & return to him		1 C 16:10-11

DATE	EVENT	ACTS	LETTERS
	Paul plans to stay in Ephesus at least till Pentecost, 53		1 C 16:8
	Paul plans to then visit Macedonia & perhaps winter in Corinth	19:21	1 C 16:5-6 1 C 16:6; cf. 16:3-4
	Paul plans to then leave Corinth for wherever, perhaps Jerusalem or Rome		1 C 16:8
c. Mar. 53	Paul writes 1 Corinthians from Ephesus	19:21	
c. Apr. 53	Timothy returns; perhaps his report responsible for Paul's change of plans		
	Paul now plans to visit Corinth first, then Macedonia, then Corinth again, then to Judea		2 C 1:16
May–Oct. 53	Paul stays awhile in Ephesus (till Pentecost), then departs for Macedonia (via Corinth)	19:22 20:1	(1 C 16:8) (2 C 1:16) 2 C 2:1
	Paul's visit to Corinth is painful		
	Paul goes on to Macedonia *as he planned*, & perhaps Illyricum	20:2	cf. R 15:19
	Paul no longer plans to return to Corinth from Macedonia as it would only be painful		2 C 1:23–2:1
	Paul writes a tearful letter to Corinth & sends it with Titus		2 C 2:3-11

DATE	EVENT	ACTS	LETTERS
	Paul apparently plans to meet Titus at Troas (Titus would sail across)		2 C 2:12-13
Oct.–Nov. 53	Paul does not find Titus at Troas		
Nov. 11, 53	Sailing season ends for winter		
Late Nov. 53	Paul goes into Macedonia looking for Titus who must now come by land		2 C 2:13
Dec. 53	Paul finds Titus in Macedonia & is greatly encouraged		2 C 7:6-7
	Paul & Timothy write 2 Corinthians from Macedonia & send with Titus		2 C 1:1; 7:5-6; 8:1; 9:2-4
	Paul plans to make a third visit to Corinth to pick up the collection		2 C 12:14; 13:1; 9:3-5
Jan.–Mar. 54	Paul visits Corinth & stays 3 months in Greece	20:3	
	Paul writes Romans from Corinth		(cf. 1 C 16:6) R 16:23
	Paul plans to leave Corinth for Syria & Jerusalem with the contribution, then to Rome, then to Spain	20:3	R 15:24-28
	Plot by Jews forces another change in plans; Paul sends most of his companions on to Troas; Paul & Luke return through Macedonia	20:3-6	

DATE	EVENT	ACTS	LETTERS
Apr. 12–19, 54	Passover and Unleavened Bread	20:6	
Apr. 23, 54	Paul & Luke sail from Philippi	20:6	
May 4, 54	Paul in Troas on Sunday	20:7	
	Paul hopes to reach Jerusalem by Pentecost	20:16	
May 31, 54	Pentecost		
	Paul's Sixth Jerusalem Visit (arrest visit)	21:15–23:31	
June 54–May 56	**Paul in Prison in Caesarea**	23:33–26:32	
	Felix leaves Paul in prison for 2 years	24:27	
May 56	Festus arrives in Caesarea	24:27	
Summer 56–Feb. 57	**Paul's Shipwrecked Journey to Rome**	27:1–28:16	
Oct. 9, 56	Day of Atonement (the Fast)	27:9	
Nov. 11, 56–Feb. 8, 57	Paul on Malta for the 3 months of the non-sailing season	28:11	
Feb. 57–c. Feb. 59	**Paul's First Roman Imprisonment**	28:14-31	
	Paul under guard 2 whole years	28:16, 30	
c. 58	Paul writes Philippians, Philemon, Colossians, & Ephesians		
	Paul plans to send Timothy to Philippi & back		Php 2:19

DATE	EVENT	ACTS	LETTERS
	Paul hopes to visit Philippi soon		Php 2:24
	Paul plans to visit Philemon		Phm 22
59–67	**Paul's Later Travels**		
59	Paul sails from Rome to Crete & leaves Titus		T 1:5
	Paul crosses to Asia & visits Philemon at Colossae		Phm 22
	On way to Macedonia, Paul exhorts Timothy to remain in Ephesus		1 Tm 1:3
c. 60	Paul visits Philippi		Php 2:24
c. 61–65	Paul goes to Spain		cf. R 15:24, 28
Early–Mid 65	Paul writes 1 Timothy; hopes to visit Timothy soon but may be delayed		1 Tm 3:14-15
Mid 65	Paul writes Titus; wants Titus to join him at Nicopolis where he will spend the winter		T 3:12
Winter 65–66	Paul at Nicopolis		T 3:12
66	Paul visits Corinth		2 Tm 4:20
	Paul visits Miletus		2 Tm 4:20
Sept. 66–Jan. 68	Nero travels in Greece		
Late 66–Early 67	Paul arrested in Troas		2 Tm 4:13
c. 67	Paul's Second Roman Imprisonment		2 Tm 1:16-17
	Paul's martyrdom is imminent		2 Tm 4:6

DATE	EVENT	ACTS	LETTERS
Mid 67	Paul writes 2 Timothy Paul wants Timothy to come soon, before winter		2 Tm 4:9, 21
c. Winter 67–68	Paul martyred in Rome		